Alice McDermott

What About the Baby?

Alice McDermott is the author of eight novels, including
The Ninth Hour; *Someone*; *After This*; *Charming Billy*,
winner of the 1998 National Book Award; *At Weddings
and Wakes*; and *That Night*—all published by FSG. *That
Night*, *At Weddings and Wakes*, and *After This* were final-
ists for the Pulitzer Prize. Her stories and essays have appeared in *The New York Times*, *The Washington Post*, *The
New Yorker*, *Harper's Magazine*, and other publications.
For more than two decades she was the Richard A. Mack-
sey Professor for Distinguished Teaching in the Human-
ities at Johns Hopkins University and a member of the
faculty at the Sewanee Writers' Conference. McDermott
lives with her family outside Washington, D.C.

ALSO BY ALICE McDERMOTT

What About the Baby?

What About the Baby?

SOME THOUGHTS

ON THE ART OF

FICTION

ALICE McDERMOTT

Picador   Farrar, Straus and Giroux   New York

Picador
120 Broadway, New York 10271

Printed in the United States of America
Originally published in 2021 by Farrar, Straus and Giroux
First paperback edition, 2022

Owing to limitations of space, all acknowledgments for permission to reprint
previously published material can be found on pages 241–242.

The Library of Congress has cataloged the Farrar, Straus and Giroux hardcover
edition as follows:
Names: McDermott, Alice, author.
Title: What about the baby? : some thoughts on the art of fiction / Alice McDermott.
Description: First edition. | New York : Farrar, Straus and Giroux, 2021.
Identifiers: LCCN 2021011633 | ISBN 9780374130626 (hardcover)
Subjects: LCSH: Fiction—Authorship. | LCGFT: Essays.
Classification: LCC PS3563.C355 W48 2021 | DDC 814/.54—dc23
LC record available at https://lccn.loc.gov/2021011633

Paperback ISBN: 978-1-250-84922-9

Designed by Abby Kagan

Surely we do better to acknowledge that literature, like language, is seldom simply but always also about itself.

—JOHN BARTH, "The Title of This Book"

CONTENTS

FOREWORD

Alice McDermott Speaks in Italics
BY TONY EARLEY

Alice McDermott and I have taught together at the Sewanee Writers' Conference so many times that we've become the workshop equivalent of an old married couple. We speak in the private code of the long familiar. During class, if she says, "Tell them about that thing . . . ," I know what thing she means. When I move my hand half an inch toward her on the tabletop, she knows it's time to move on to the next story. And when she purses her lips and makes a noise, audible only to me, that sounds like the last flight of a disappointed mosquito, I know I've said something stupid. I stop talking and look at her and say, "What?"

She says, "Well . . . ," before suggesting, in the politest possible terms, that what I just said, while not exactly stupid, is perhaps not all that bright. She suggests an alternative. She is never wrong.

I look at the class and say, "What she said."

If every story has an ideal narrative line, a Platonic yellow brick road that leads to the one place where it is meant to go, the problem for the writer is that a story can go to an infinite number of other places, and the shape of that infinity changes every time the writer chooses a word. Somebody cuts off your character in traffic. My thesaurus has fifty-one words for *angry*. Pick one. The stars rearrange themselves in the sky. Alice is a genius at peering into that cacophony of possibility and seeing the ideal line.

Say an orthopedic appliance salesman from St. Louis named Steve submits a story to our workshop about an orthopedic appliance salesman from East St. Louis named Bill. Bill's company is losing its artificial-knee market share to a Chinese conglomerate; his wife has begun taking yoga classes; they fight about the pants; he stops at McDonald's to get coffee and remembers the toy train set the two of them put together one Christmas for their now estranged son; Bill resolves to dig the train out of the garage and make it run again.

Steve reads a page from his story aloud and looks up expectantly. Alice asks for comments. A woman asks, Why only knees? Maybe Bill could sell hips, too? The retired army guy speculates about what is wrong with the train. The woman from New York wonders if it's racist that the knees putting Bill out of business were made in China.

"Knees," Alice says. "Titanium. Not titanium. American. Chinese. Who cares? It doesn't matter. Bill could be selling dynamite to coyotes. What's the *story*?" I have no idea what she's talking about, only that she has begun speaking in italics. I help her stare down the room. Nobody answers.

"What about the clairvoyant sword swallower?" Alice asks.

Clairvoyant sword swallower? I look down at my manuscript. What clairvoyant sword swallower?

"Page eleven," Alice says. Sure enough, on page eleven, halfway down, a clairvoyant sword swallower materializes in a haze of coffee steam. She reads palms in a storefront in a dingy strip mall across the highway from McDonald's. Every morning she watches the sad guy drinking coffee. Because she's clairvoyant, she knows about the knees and the wife and the yoga and the pants and the train. She knows that today Bill will drive over and ask what happened to the model-train store that used to be there. She'll read his palm, but she already knows that the Chinese knees will cost him his job, that his wife will pack up her yoga pants and move out, that she gave the toy train to Goodwill when their son went away to college. He will stare at the swords hanging on the wall but be too shy to ask.

Alice leans forward. "The sword-swallowing clairvoyant will know all this," she says, "but guess what? She. Won't. Tell. Him. A. Thing." She taps the manuscript again. "And *that*," she says, "is the *story*."

Everyone in the class is scribbling furiously. Underlining. Steve is about to weep with joy. Oh, thank you, Alice, he says. Thank you so much. Turns out his grandmother was a clairvoyant sword swallower. Sword swallowing is how she saved enough money to sneak her children out of the Old Country. Clairvoyance is how they made it through the mines and the wire and the searchlights and over the wall. In America she worked the boardwalk seven days a week. Sent everybody to college. Died before Steve was born. Swallowed one sword too many. She knew it was coming. Steve says, I never really wanted to write about artificial knees, but I thought knees were all I knew. But now, he says—he takes a minute to compose himself—now I know the *story*.

I'm still staring at my copy of the manuscript, wondering how the hell I missed a clairvoyant sword swallower.

Alice turns to me and smiles, asks, "Do you want to add anything?"

I smile back. Right now I'm the luckiest man on the mountain. I'm sitting at a table with *Alice McDermott*.

"Nope," I say. "We're good."

What About the Baby?

WHAT I EXPECT

On June 17, 2001, three New York City firemen were killed while fighting a Sunday afternoon fire in a hardware store in Astoria, Queens. Apparently, an illegally stored propane tank caused the explosion that toppled a brick wall onto two of the men and dropped the third through the first floor and into the basement, where he signaled for help but could not be reached before his oxygen ran out.

All three men were middle-aged Irish Catholics, longtime members of the fire department. One had been cited for bravery so often that the members of his company called any dangerous and heroic act performed by anyone a "Harry Fordism." His comrades placed in his coffin a can of beer, a stuffed bear in a Yankees T-shirt, and the *New York Times* crossword puzzle he had left unfinished when he responded to the alarm. Another was a big, cheerful guy with a remarkable sense of humor and a way with words—a teacher and mentor to young firemen. The third was to leave for Ireland the next day for a four-week vacation with his wife and two small children.

The three men had eight children among them. Each man worked a second job to supplement his fire department salary.

Had the hardware store been open, as it usually was on

Sundays, chances are good that the fire would never have started. Investigators later determined that its initial cause was some gasoline spilled under a delivery door by two neighborhood kids playing in the deserted backyard. When the gasoline hit the basement water heater, the fire began. When the fire reached the propane tank, the deadly explosion occurred.

But the owner of the store had impulsively decided to close that Sunday because it was Father's Day.

I was visiting Long Island at the time and like many other New Yorkers had this account provided to me by the New York *Daily News*: three days of front-page stories filled with the sad, ironic, heroic details, as well as the familiar photographs—official fire department portraits and grinning photos of the men among their children, and then the orderly rows of firefighters outside the various churches, the flag-draped coffins on the fire trucks, the sobbing eight-year-old clutching his father's helmet.

And all the while the newspaper was filled with these details and these photographs, before it moved on to other front-page stories about Mayor Giuliani's awkward love life and the five children murdered by their mother in Texas, I found myself recalling, and longing to reread, Mark Helprin's very short story "White Gardens." I wanted to reread the story though I hadn't looked at it in years, not merely for a chance to ponder a fictional retelling of a similar event, not even for a chance to see real life's cold ironies put to better use, but simply to hear again the beauty of its language, the rhythm of its sentences. To glimpse again the moment the story describes.

This is how it goes:

It was August. In the middle of his eulogy the priest said, "Now they must leave us, to repose in white gardens," and then halted in confusion, for he had certainly meant green gardens. But he was not sure. No one in the overcrowded church knew what he meant by white gardens instead of green, but they felt that the mistake was in some way appropriate, and most of them would remember for the rest of their lives the moment afterward, when he had glanced at them in alarm and puzzlement.

The stone church in Brooklyn, on one of the long avenues stretching to the sea, was full of firefighters, the press, uncharacteristically quiet city politicians in tropical suits, and the wives and eighteen children of the six men who, in the blink of an eye, had dropped together through the collapsing roof of a burning building, deep into an all-consuming firestorm.

Everyone noticed that the wives of the firemen who had died looked exceptionally beautiful. The young women—with the golden hair of summer, in dark print dresses—several of whom carried flowers, and the older, more matronly women who were less restrained because they understood better what was to become of them, all had a frightening, elevated quality which seemed to rule the parishioners and silence the politicians.

The priest was tumbling over his own words, perhaps because he was young and too moved to be eloquent according to convention. He looked up after a long silence and said, simply, "repose of rivers . . ." They strained to understand, but couldn't, and forgave him immediately. His voice was breaking—not because so many were in the church, for in the raw shadow of the event itself, their numbers were unimpressive. It wasn't that the Mayor was in the crowd: the Mayor had become just a man, and no one felt the power of his office. It may have been the heat. The city had been under siege for a week. Key West humidity and rains had swept across Brooklyn, never-ending, trying to cover it with the sea. The sun was shining now, through a powerful white haze, and the heat inside the church was phenomenal and frightening, ninety-five degrees—like a boiler room. All the seasons have their mystery, and perhaps the mystery of summer is that it overwhelms with easy life, and makes one feel improperly immortal.

One of the wives glanced out a high window and saw white smoke billowing from a chimney. Even in this kind of weather, she thought, they have to turn on the furnaces to make hot water. The smoke rushed past the masonry as if the chimney were the stack of a ship. She had been to a fireman's funeral before, and she knew what it was going to be like when the flag-draped coffin was borne from the church and placed on the bed of a shiny new engine. Hundreds of uniformed men would snap to attention, their blue hats aligning suddenly. Then the procession would flow away like a blue river, and she, the widow (for she was now the widow), would stagger into a waiting black car to follow after it.

She was one of the younger wives, one of those who were filled with restrained motion, one of the ones in a dark print dress with flowers. She was looking to the priest for direction, but he was coming apart, and as he did she could not keep out of her mind the million things she was thinking, the things which came to her for no reason, just the way the priest had said "white gardens," and "repose of rivers." She thought of the barges moving slowly up the Hudson in a tunnel of silver and white haze, and of the wind-polished bridges standing in the summer sun. She thought of the men in the church. She knew them. They were firefighters; they were rough, and they carried with them in the church more ambition, sadness, power, courage, greed, and anger than she cared to think about on this day. But despite their battalion's worth of liveliness and strength, they were drawn to the frail priest whose voice broke every now and then in the presence of the wives and the children and the six coffins.

She thought of Brooklyn, of its vastness, and of the things that were happening in Brooklyn, right then. Even as the men were buried, traffic on the streets and parkways would be thick as blood; a hundred million emotions would pass from soul to soul, into the air, into walls in dark hot rooms, into thin groves of trees in the parks. Even as the men were buried in an emerald field dazzling with row upon row of bone-white gravestones, there would be something of resurrection and life all over Brooklyn. But now it was still, and the priest was lost in a moment during which everyone was brought together, and the suited children and lovely wives learned that there are quiet times when the world is touched, and when that which is truly important arises to claim all allegiances.

"It is bitter," said the priest, finally in control of himself, "bitter that only through windows like these do we see clearly into past and future, that in such scenes we burn through our temporal concerns to see that everything that was, is; and that everything that is, will always be." She looked at him, bending her head slightly and pursing her lips in an expression of love and sadness, and he continued. "For we shall always have green gardens, and we shall always have white gardens, too."

Now they knew what he meant, and it shot like electricity through the six wives, the eighteen children, and the blue river of men.

I expect a lot of fiction—of mine and yours and everybody else's. My need to reread this story in the light of these three men's deaths, not simply to recall it or to remember its similarities or to describe it to somebody else, but to reread the story itself—a kind of antidote—might be evidence of this.

Helprin's brief story is not an antidote, of course, to the heartache, the cold and useless ironies of that Sunday afternoon fire in Queens; and yet there is solace in the reading of it, because the language is clear and the images are fine and the story's few brief platitudes seem both true and appropriate—*earned*, as we say in writing workshops—by the language and the images and the circumstances of the tale. But more than this, "White Gardens" offers solace because among the many insults contained in the real-life story of that fire in Queens is the indisputable fact that time will move us all away from it, *has* moved us all away from it—not just the front-page editors at the *Daily News*, but the readers of newspapers, the eulogizing politicians, the other firefighters, even the wives and the children, the weeping eight-year-old.

Time will move us away from the sad circumstances of the deaths of three good men, dull the outrage as well as the pain, dull the grief, too.

And yet, the moment Helprin describes in "White Gardens" remains vivid and unchanged.

The heat bears down on the mourners, and the young wife sees the white smoke billowing from the chimney, and the firemen, "despite their battalion's worth of liveliness and strength," look to the frail priest *endlessly*, not because the moment itself takes place out of time but because the story exists out of time, unchanging, enduring, there for the reading and the rereading for what is, as far as most of us are concerned, forever.

It's the solace of art, I suppose. Art in its "Ode on a Grecian Urn" mode. Art that arrests time, tames it, preserves our heartache or our outrage or our joy, our days on earth, from the dulling indignity of time's healing, obliterating hand.

The solace of art. Scenes that "burn through our temporal concerns."

This is what I expect of fiction.

Here's a similar moment in Toni Morrison's *Song of Solomon*:

Two days later, halfway through the service, it seemed as though Ruth was going to be the lone member of the bereaved family there. A female quartet from Linden Baptist Church had already sung "Abide With Me"; the wife of the mortician had read the condolence cards and the minister had launched into his "Naked came ye into this life and naked shall ye depart" sermon, which he had always believed suitable for the death of a young woman; and the winos in the vestibule who came to pay their respects to "Pilate's girl," but who dared not enter, had begun to sob, when the door swung open and Pilate burst in, shouting, "Mercy!" as though it were a command. A young man stood up and moved toward her. She flung out her right arm and almost knocked him down. "I want mercy!" she shouted, and began walking toward the coffin, shaking her head from side to side to side as though somebody had asked her a question and her answer was no.

Halfway up the aisle she stopped, lifted a finger, and pointed. Then slowly, although her breathing was fast and shallow, she lowered her hand to her side. It was strange, the languorous, limp hand coming to rest at her side while her breathing was coming so quick and fast. "Mercy," she said again, but she whispered it now. The mortician scurried toward her and touched her elbow. She moved away from him and went right up to the bier. She tilted her head and looked down. Her earring grazed her shoulder. Out of the total blackness of her clothes it blazed like a star. The mortician tried to approach her again, and moved closer, but when he saw her inky, berry-black lips, her cloudy, rainy eyes, the wonderful brass box hanging from her ear, he stepped back and looked at the floor.

"Mercy?" Now she was asking a question. "Mercy?"

It was not enough. The word needed a bottom, a frame. She straightened up, held her head high, and transformed the plea into a note. In a clear bluebell voice she sang it out—the one word held so long it became a sentence—and before the last syllable had died in the corners of the room, she was answered in sweet soprano: "I hear you."

Stories we return to not so much for solace as for the way the moment, the sentiment—fleeting tragedy, fleeting triumph—is made fully retrievable, forever, by language, by art: this is what I expect of fiction.

Which is not to say that I expect only funerals in fiction—although I must confess to a certain, possibly genetic, fondness for funerals. Time's dulling effect can do its obliterating work on pleasure as well as pain, and I expect the fiction I read to recognize joy in all its gradations and complications, in its longevity and brevity, as vividly as it recognizes sorrow. I think of Saul Bellow's Ravelstein: "Writers," he says, "are supposed to make you laugh and cry. It's what mankind is looking for."

I think of John Cheever:

My name is Johnny Hake. I'm thirty-six years old, stand five feet eleven in my socks, weigh one hundred and forty-two pounds stripped, and am, so to speak, naked at the moment and talking into the dark. I was conceived in the Hotel St. Regis, born in the Presbyterian Hospital, raised on Sutton Place, christened and confirmed in St. Bartholomew's, and I drilled with the Knickerbocker Greys, played football and baseball in Central Park, learned to chin myself on the framework of East Side apartment-house canopies, and met my wife (Christina

Lewis) at one of the big cotillions at the Waldorf. I served four years in the Navy, have four kids now, and live in a *banlieue* called Shady Hill. We have a nice house with a garden and a place outside for cooking meat, and on summer nights, sitting there with the kids and looking into the front of Christina's dress as she bends over to salt the steaks, or just gazing at the lights in heaven, I am as thrilled as I am thrilled by more hardy and dangerous pursuits, and I guess this is what is meant by the pain and sweetness of life.

I expect fiction to be about the pain and sweetness of life.

I expect fictional narrators to stand naked, talking into the dark, so that the words they choose are neither self-conscious or self-serving nor—worse yet—author-conscious or author-serving but direct and honest and as true as they can make them.

And then Ricky begins. What will it be this time, I think. I am wild with anticipation. Whatever it will be, I know it is all anyone in the world can give me now—perhaps the most anyone has ever been able to give a man like me. As Ricky begins, I try to think of all the good things the other children have done for me through the years and of their affection, and of my wife's. But it seems this was all there ever was. I forget my pains and my pills, and the canceled golf game, and the meaningless mail of the morning. I find I can scarcely sit still in my chair for wanting Ricky to get on with it. Has he been brandishing his pistol again? Or dragging the sheriff's deputy across a field at midnight? And does he have in his wallet perhaps a picture of some other girl with a tight little mouth, and eyes that burn? Will his outrageous story include her? And perhaps explain it, leaving her a blessed mystery? As Ricky begins, I find myself

listening not merely with fixed attention but with my whole
being . . . I hear him beginning. I am listening. I am listening
gratefully to all he will tell me about himself, about any life that
is not my own.

—PETER TAYLOR, "THE GIFT OF THE PRODIGAL"

I expect fiction to be about lives that are not my own.

And yet I expect fiction to be truer than life—yours, mine,
everybody else's—truer than reportage, lecture, memoir, or sermon, so that we, its readers, might listen with our whole being.

I get my fill of vacuity from real-life discourse, thank you. I
get my fill of veiled insincerity, selfishness, manipulation, too. It
is enough of an effort to excuse one another's blind egotism in
daily life. I don't expect to have to make excuses for an author's
blind egotism while I'm reading a work of fiction.

In *The Counterlife*, Philip Roth lets one of his characters,
Henry Zuckerman, a successful oral surgeon and the younger
brother of famous writer Nathan Zuckerman, read a chapter
from Nathan's latest novel, a chapter we readers have already
read, the first chapter of the book we hold. The chapter is told
from a fictionalized "Henry Zuckerman's" point of view, and
so we are privy to the "real" Henry's reaction to his brother's
portrait—a portrait we readers have accepted, just a hundred
pages before, as truth.

. . . it occurred to Henry that Nathan's deepest satisfaction
as a writer must have derived from these perverse distortions
of truth, as though he wrote to distort, for that pleasure pri-
marily, and only incidentally to malign. No mind on earth
could have been more alien than the mind revealed to him
by this book . . . Exaggeration. Exaggeration, falsification,
rampant caricature—everything, thought Henry, about my

vocation, to which precision, accuracy, mechanical exactness are absolutely essential, overstated, overdrawn, and vulgarly enlarged . . . I am a success, Nathan. I don't live all day vicariously in my head—I live with saliva, blood, bone, teeth, my hands in mouths as raw and real as the meat in the butcher's window!

I expect all characters in fiction to insist on their own authenticity as vehemently as Henry demands it of Nathan, to stand in judgment of their author's loyalty to the truth of their lives as passionately as Henry does, to resist caricature and to contradict, if need be, their own creator's easy assessment—no matter how conveniently that assessment serves story or plot—by shouting words like "saliva, blood, bone, teeth," and, most essential, "I am."

I expect this because I want the fiction I read not only to recognize the infinite value and variety and worth inherent in the human soul, the human character, I want it to help me to believe in this infinite variety and value when "real" life seems so determined to prove otherwise. I want to believe that we human beings are, all of us, of equal value and depth and complexity when we stand naked talking into the dark despite how readily, hourly, life presents us with fellow human beings who make us doubt this premise—fellow human beings we suspect we would prefer never to hear or to see in such circumstances (naked, that is, talking into the dark).

I expect fiction never to cave in to these suspicions. I expect fiction to reject one-dimensional characters, easy stereotypes, ready-to-hand clichés, to contain, consistently, characters who, if they don't shine with the light of their uniquely individual souls, shimmer at least with that soul's unplumbed or as yet unillustrated possibilities.

In her introduction to her collected stories, Eudora Welty writes:

> I have been told, both in approval and in accusation, that I seem to love all my characters. What I do in writing of any character is to try to enter into the mind, heart, and skin of a human being who is not myself. Whether this happens to be a man or a woman, old or young, with skin black or white, the primary challenge lies in making the jump itself. It is the act of a writer's imagination that I set most high.

I expect authors to love their characters.

But that's not to say that I expect all characters to be lovable, or even likeable. Consider this marvelous passage:

> The road now stretched across open country, and it occurred to me—not by way of protest, not as a symbol, or anything like that, but merely as a novel exercise—that since I had disregarded all laws of humanity, I might as well disregard the rules of traffic. So I crossed to the left side of the highway and checked the feeling, and the feeling was good. It was a pleasant diaphragmal melting, with elements of diffused tactility, all this enhanced by the thought that nothing could be nearer to the elimination of basic physical laws than deliberately driving on the wrong side of the road. In a way, it was a very spiritual itch. Gently, dreamily, not exceeding twenty miles an hour, I drove on that queer mirror side. Traffic was light. Cars that now and then passed me on the side I had abandoned to them, honked at me brutally. Cars coming toward me wobbled, swerved, cried out in fear. Presently I found myself approaching populated places. Passing through a red light was like a sip of forbidden Burgundy when I was a child. Meanwhile, com-

plications were arising. I was being followed and escorted. Then in front of me I saw two cars placing themselves in such a manner as to completely block my way. With graceful movement I turned off the road, and after two or three big bounces, rode up a grassy slope, among surprised cows, and there I came to a gentle rocking stop.

Write me a line like "Passing through a red light was like a sip of forbidden Burgundy when I was a child," and I'll take Humbert Humbert into my head and into my heart. I'll love him in all his awful, complex humanity, see him as one of our own, because I recognize something in his words—some delight, some humor, some essential memory—that tells me he is indeed one of us, even in all his awfulness. Our awfulness.

Something in his words. Because if words be made of breath and breath of life, then I expect wonderful words from the fiction I read. Story is one thing—yes, sure, we all expect some kind of story. And character, sure. But story is ubiquitous, and characters, too; the *Daily News* and *The New York Times* are full of stories and characters, as are network and cable TV, cocktail parties, family reunions. It is the careful, original, felicitous use of language that is rare and wondrous.

I expect the language in fiction not merely to tell a story and to create a character and to place that character in a particular moment that obliterates time; language in fiction must also record, re-create, what is intuited but never heard, sensed but never experienced. Language in fiction is obliged to invoke what cannot be said, what Virginia Woolf called in *To the Lighthouse* "the voice of the beauty of the world."

Through the open window the voice of the beauty of the world came murmuring, too softly to hear exactly what it said—but what mattered if the meaning were plain?—entreating the sleepers (the house was full again; Mrs. Beckwith was staying there, also Mr. Carmichael), if they would not actually come down to the beach itself at least to lift the blind and look out. They would see then night flowing down in purple; his head crowned; his sceptre jewelled; and how in his eyes a child might look. And if they still faltered (Lily was tired out with travelling and slept almost at once; but Mr. Carmichael read a book by candlelight), if they still said no, that it was vapour, this splendour of his, and the dew had more power than he, and they preferred sleeping; gently then, without complaint, or argument, the voice would sing its song.

I expect the fiction I read to replicate, each story in its own way, the voice of the beauty of the world and to do it with just such humility and courage. I mean the humility and courage it takes to say, "What matter if the meaning were plain?" or "What matter if the world falter and refuse to hear?" I expect the fiction I read to carry with it the conviction that it is written with no other incentive than that it must be written. I expect the fiction I read to conform to that favorite word of dust-jacket copywriters worldwide: *compelling*, but with the understanding that both writer and reader are compelled equally—by a story told for no other reason than that it must be told, just as it must be read.

Echoes of Rosa Coldfield in the opening scene of *Absalom, Absalom!*:

"Because you are going away to attend the college at Harvard they tell me," Miss Coldfield said. "So I don't imagine you will ever come back here and settle down as a country lawyer in a little town like Jefferson, since Northern people have already seen to it that there is little left in the South for a young man. So maybe you will enter the literary profession as so many Southern gentlemen and gentlewomen too are doing now and maybe some day you will remember this and write about it. You will be married then I expect and perhaps your wife will want a new gown or a new chair for the house and you can write this and submit it to the magazines. Perhaps you will even remember kindly then the old woman who made you spend a whole afternoon sitting indoors and listening while she talked about people and events you were fortunate enough to escape yourself when you wanted to be out among young friends of your own age."

"Yessum," Quentin said. Only she don't mean that, he thought. It's because she wants it told.

I expect the fiction I read to be memorable. It is probably the most elementary of measures, but it is one I can't help but apply, because it's so delightful when it happens—when a line or a character or a moment, a turn of phrase or the perfect shape of a chapter, an entire book—returns to you hours, days, maybe months or years after you've done the reading, when you recognize that the phrase, the line, the scene, the story has become part of your own experience of life, part of the fabric of your own thought. I expect the fiction I read to come back to me—unbidden sometimes, a lovely refrain, apropos of nothing, a pleasure recalled. I expect it to come back to me, as well, in response to life's cold ironies—three good men killed in a Father's Day fire—in response to time's indifference, or to our own immeasurable failings, yours, mine, and everybody else's. I expect the fiction I read to make its rereading a necessity.

Just three months after those firefighters were killed in Astoria, the twin towers came down, and 343 New York firefighters lost their lives—far more than a battalion's worth of liveliness and strength. In the days and weeks that followed, I made note of how often I heard poetry quoted in the public square, on radio and television and in the speeches of politicians. Auden and Yeats and Dickinson and Whitman. Shakespeare, too, and even some prose—lines from E. B. White's *Here Is New York*, for instance. None of it written for the terrible occasion itself, but words that offered comfort nonetheless.

I was reminded of the arguments my parents used to make when I was a child, a too-thin-for-their-liking, "picky-eater" of a child: You should always carry a few extra pounds, they told me, in case you get sick and can't eat. A few extra pounds to fall back on. It was a logic gained, no doubt, during their own Depression-era childhoods, but in those awful post–9/11 days it made me think about the poet's, the writer's, obligation to be memorable. To offer us readers words that might be woven into the fabric of our own thoughts, our own memories, so we can find them again, fall back on them, when experience, life's cruelties, leaves us with nothing to say.

Little wonder that both Helprin and Morrison, in depicting grief, illustrate, too, the frustrating inadequacy of language. "It was not enough." And yet it's all we've got.

I expect fiction to be inspired.

My son was a sophomore in high school when he related to me one night the discussion they'd had in his English class that day, the inevitable discussion about whether Shakespeare was the true author of all those plays or whether they'd been written by some better-educated nobleman or playwright or some consortium of noblemen and playwrights—the familiar debate. I have to confess, I was only half listening—it was a weeknight, and my other two kids still had homework to finish, and I had laundry to do and student papers to read—and so when he asked me who I thought Shakespeare really was, I said without thinking, "I think he was an angel."

It was only when he replied, with healthy skepticism, "Are you serious?" that I realized I probably was.

Somewhere in my hopeful heart or deluded mind, I harbor a belief in Divine Inspiration. This may be some tattered fragment of my Catholic education. It is most certainly not a product of my own experience. I recall, in fact, the very first time I was asked to be on a panel of fiction writers, shortly after I'd published my first novel. I was onstage with an older, august author of international reputation and another first novelist, newly celebrated. A question came from the audience (it would prove to be a recurring one): "Where do you get your ideas?" And the August Presence replied without hesitation, "From the Holy Spirit." My fellow first novelist nodded eagerly. "Me, too," she said. "The Holy Spirit."

It was my first intimation that I had chosen the wrong profession.

No tongues of fire had scorched my scalp during the creation of my first novel or, for that matter, any novel since.

As a reader, though, I buy the assertion wholeheartedly. The Holy Spirit, the Muse, Divine Inspiration. Think about it: Our need for fiction is not biological; it's not even practical. We no longer need stories to tell us how to avoid being eaten by a saber-toothed tiger. We no longer need stories to explain to us—in terms we can understand, huddled in the dark, hoping the sun will return—the workings of the natural world. Certainly, we no longer need stories to show us how to save our immortal souls.

And yet our need for fiction, our longing for fiction (not to mention our making of fiction), persists. I suppose you could argue that this need is indeed only some vestige of that earlier, primitive, practical habit of mind, that it is some appendix or tailbone of the brain or of the heart that evolution, our growing sophistication, our vast knowledge, has made obsolete. But such an argument hardly accounts for the complexity, the variety, the sheer volume of story we humans produce, or for the relentless way we continue to produce it, to seek it out, to fold it into our experience and our memories.

I'm with Faulkner when he claims that literature is not merely the record of man's puny, inexhaustible voice but one of the pillars and props of humanity itself. I'm with Harold Bloom when he claims that Shakespeare did not merely illustrate what it is to be human, he invented it, brought our complex humanity into being by revealing it to ourselves. I'm with the wide and motley cast of authors I have heard extoll the beauty of Mark's Gospel or of Genesis, of the Old and New Testaments as a whole—Barry Hannah, Min Jin Lee, Marilynne Robinson, Reynolds Price come immediately to mind—and I am unwilling to believe that the Creator, having dabbled in the writer's craft then, would have abandoned that craft to us amateurs for the next two thousand years.

I find it a matter of simple logic that if we novelists have, over all these centuries, used our literature to send our appeals, our laments, our complaints—as well as our observations on the pain and sweetness of life—to the Powers That Be, then surely the Powers That Be must, on occasion, answer in kind.

I expect fiction to be that answer in kind.

Finally, lest we forget: I expect fiction to be a continual source of surprise and delight. I expect to be surprised and delighted every time I read a new work, whether its author is a literary icon or a student writer completing a first draft, just as I expect to be surprised and delighted all over again every time I return to something familiar.

I don't accept the desert-island mentality. (I don't much like

Best Books lists either. Rank rankings.) Who among us wants to settle for one book, one author, one voice? I like the way David Lodge puts this at the end of his novel *Souls and Bodies*. His words are an exegesis on faith, but faith is, of course, exactly what we talk about when we talk about what we expect:

> We must not only believe, but know that we believe, live our belief and yet see it from the outside, aware that in another time, another place, we would have believed something different (indeed did ourselves believe differently at different times and places in our lives) without feeling that this invalidates belief. Just as when reading a novel, or writing one for that matter, we maintain a double consciousness of the characters as both, as it were, real and fictitious, free and determined, and know that however absorbing and convincing we may find it, it is not the only story we shall want to read (or, as the case may be, write) but part of an endless sequence of stories by which man has sought and will always seek to make sense of life. And death.

I expect fiction to seek to make sense of life and death— yours, mine, and everybody else's.

STORY

An old man wakes up one morning, calls to his dog, and heads out on a lovely walk down a familiar country road.

As the two go along leisurely, enjoying the scenery and the fine weather, the old man slowly begins to recall that the dog at his side died many years ago, when the old man himself was just leaving his boyhood. Delighted as he is to see his dog again, the man can't help but conclude that if this friend of his youth has returned to him, then he, too, must have died. And indeed, as he walks, the old man remembers his own peaceful passing.

Soon enough, man and dog come to a turn in the road that leads up a steep hill. At the top of the hill, the man can just glimpse a towering white arch lit up with the sun. As he and his dog approach, the old man sees, as well, high, alabaster walls inlaid with mother-of-pearl, and then two golden gates, and, behind them, a street paved with gold. There's a handsome man sitting at a beautiful desk just inside the gate.

"Is this heaven?" the old man asks.

"Yes, it is," the man at the desk says. "Would you like to come in?"

"I would indeed," the old man replies.

Smiling warmly, the gatekeeper rises from the desk. "And is there anything we can get for you?" he asks as he comes forward to open the gate.

"Well, I've been walking a long time," the old man says. "I'd love a drink of water."

The man says he'll gladly have a glass of ice water sent right up.

"And have you got a bowl for the dog?" the old man asks.

The gatekeeper pauses behind the gate, his hand frozen on the latch. "Oh, the dog can't come in," he says. "Pets aren't allowed here."

The old man looks at the handsome fellow behind the gate and the street of gold beyond him. He looks up at the sunlight on the beautiful arch and down at his dog.

"I'll be going along, then," the old man says, and he turns and walks back down the hill and out onto the road.

The man and the dog continue in the direction they had been going.

After another long walk, they reach the top of another steep hill, where they find a dirt road that leads through a farm gate. There's no fence, and the gate is wide open. So much grass has grown up around the gate that it looks as though it's never been closed. Just beyond the gate, there's a man sitting in a rickety chair in the shade of a tree, reading a book. The old man calls to him, "Excuse me, sir. Sorry to bother, but I've been walking a long time, and I wonder if you've got any water."

The man looks up from his book. "Oh, sure," he says. "There's a pump over there." And he points to a place beyond the gate. "Come in and help yourself."

But as the old man approaches the farm gate, he hesitates. "What about my friend here?" he asks, gesturing toward his dog.

The man returns to his book. "Not a problem," he says pleasantly. "There's a bowl beside the pump."

The old man and his dog pass through the gate, and, sure enough, they find the water pump. The old man fills the bowl for his dog and then takes a long drink himself.

The two return to thank the man. They find him waiting for them in the shade of the tree.

"This is a very nice place," the old man says.

"Yes, it is," the man under the tree says. "It's heaven, in fact."

The old man and his dog exchange a look. "Well, that's strange," the old man says. "There's a place down the road that calls itself heaven, as well."

The man under the tree smiles. "You mean the place with the alabaster walls and the golden gates?"

"That's right," the old man says. "It's very beautiful."

"It's hell," says the man.

"Is it, now?" the old man asks.

"It is," the man says, laughing. "Though they're always calling themselves heaven."

The old man considers this for a moment. "That must make you very angry," he says.

But the man with the book shakes his head. "No," he says. "We don't mind at all. They do us a great favor." And he leans to pat the old man's dog on the head. "They sort out for us all the people who can't be loyal to their friends."

I found this little story in an Irish magazine.

I read it—as I do a great deal of my magazine reading on a busy day—while walking up the driveway from the mailbox, the rest of the serious mail tucked under my arm, and Rufous, our labradoodle, watching my progress up and back with his big black nose pressed to the sidelight window beside our front door. I usually take Rufous for a midday walk after I get the mail, so if

I linger too long on the driveway with an opened magazine, he'll give a polite bark to remind me of my more pressing obligations.

I have, in fact, quite often had to make a choice—much like the old man in the story—between reading a magazine piece in its entirety, right there in the driveway, or putting it aside in favor of my shaggy friend. More than once I've entertained the notion that the fiction editors at *The New Yorker* should be informed each week of how well the opening paragraphs of the current short story have withstood Rufous's brown-eyed charms. If the opening paragraphs are good enough—vivid, lyrical, intriguing, funny (how many ways can a story seduce you into reading it in its entirety in one standing?)—then poor Rufous will have his walk delayed. Chances are that if the story is by the likes of Alice Munro or William Trevor or Tessa Hadley or George Saunders, poor Rufous will have his walk delayed.

Far more often, however, he will give his polite bark and then that wonderful, anticipatory, whole-body shiver that dogs do to convey their gratitude for what you haven't even done for them yet, and the story loses out. Call it the Rufous test. Do you choose the story of postadolescent angst in the life of a Brooklyn or L.A. hipster, or the tail-wagging dog? Do you finish reading this ironic tale of emotional catatonia in the overeducated, or do you put the stupid magazine down and pick up the leash?

One of the first writing classes I took was taught by a mad Scotsman who would read our weak opening paragraphs out loud and then, glaring, ask us why in the world anyone would want to take time out of his day to read any more of this. People have lives, he'd shout, people have things to do, people want to go out and have a drink.

Fortunately for Rufous that day, the little story in the Irish magazine was short enough to read in its entirety as I walked up the driveway. It was titled "Animals in Heaven," and it was placed as filler, a narrow, unsigned sidebar, in a magazine devoted to the Irish music scene: results of various competitions, impossibly adorable photos of Irish dancers, and group shots of impossibly stereotypical-looking (that is, they all look like my relatives) festival organizers and sponsors.

The magazine contained, as well, the usual (for the Irish) number of memorial essays—"We'll not see his like again" accounts of humble and generous fiddlers or pipers or singers who lived their lives dedicated to traditional Irish music. Obscure names, of course, known only to the community of Irish musicians—a community of artists, by the way, for whom fame and fortune play almost no part in their ambitions for their art. Kind of like poets.

There's a whole other lecture on what fiction writers can learn from practitioners of the obscure traditional arts, especially now that literary fiction is becoming one of them, one of the obscure traditional arts.

For instance: we hosted three "famous" Irish musicians at our house—incredible players all, marvelously talented—and after playing a couple of particularly wonderful tunes around our kitchen table, one of them wryly proclaimed, "Jesus, lads, there's *hundreds* to be made with this music! Hundreds!"

Billy McComiskey is a great Irish American button accordion player from Baltimore, one of the finest musicians on the scene, and a high school facilities manager in his day job. He was once asked by an adult student if he, the student, would ever learn to play as well as Billy. Billy asked him, "Do you like your job?" and the student said yes, he liked it very much. "Then you'll never play as well as I do," Billy growled. "I hate mine."

Perfection of the work, not of the life, as Yeats might note. Obscurity a small price to pay for the pleasure of indulging our passion, pursuing our vision, for the great gift of a life spent in service to the art that we, God knows why, cherish above all others.

And lest you think the novelist's pursuit, with all its possibilities of fame and fortune, movie deals and grand prizes, is of any more value than the homely pursuit of the obscure traditional arts, consider something else Yeats had to say:

> Last night I went to a wide place on the Kiltartan road to listen to some Irish songs . . . The voices melted into the twilight, and were mixed into the trees, and when I thought of the words they too melted away, and were mixed with the generations of men. Now it was a phrase, now it was an attitude of mind, an emotional form, that had carried my memory to older verses, or even to forgotten mythologies. I was carried so far that it was as though I came to one of the four rivers, and followed it under the wall of paradise to the roots of the trees of knowledge and of life . . . Folk art is, indeed, the oldest of the aristocracies of thought, and because it refuses what is passing and trivial, the merely clever and pretty, as certainly as the vulgar and insincere, and because it has gathered into itself the simplest and most unforgettable thoughts of generations, it is the soil where all great art is rooted.

". . . refuses what is passing and trivial, the merely clever and pretty, as certainly as the vulgar and insincere . . ." I love that.

But back to the story.

I don't need an Irish musician's self-awareness to understand why I felt compelled to read the whole of "Animals in Heaven" right there in the driveway, despite Rufous's adorable face at the window. For one, the piece was very short. For two, it had a dog in it—always a draw for me. I was one of those kids who lost sleep at night worrying about whether or not dogs could go to heaven (until a wonderful young nun assured me that taking care of the animals in heaven was the very task for which St. Francis of Assisi had been created). And it was about death—always a favorite subject. And it was sentimental. So am I.

But what I didn't understand, after I read the story and left the magazine with the rest of the mail on the table in the hall and took old Rufous for his walk, was how much I wanted to repeat the tale.

I had no idea what compelled me. It wasn't a joke—it didn't have one of those great punch lines you can't wait to deliver to someone else the moment after it's been delivered to you. Nor was it one of those bizarre or tragic internet stories that it seems we're always trading: *Did you read about that bride who . . . Did you see that story about the shark . . . Apparently there's a teenager in Memphis with . . .* stories we repeat for no more complex reason, it would seem, than our childish delight in the weird or our rubbernecking curiosity about other people's bad luck.

I can't say that I found "Animals in Heaven" a particularly astute little story, and I knew its charms were hackneyed and unsophisticated enough to make me aware of how poorly they might reflect on the literary taste of the teller. And yet I knew that if I had run into a neighbor on my walk with Rufous that day, I would have told her the whole tale as soon as I could work it into the conversation—which would have been easy enough to do, *dog* being the operative, single-word preface, and Rufous himself being the obliging narrative segue.

I know I repeated the story to my husband as we put dinner together that night. (He reacted with a tolerant, "Ah, cute.") I know I told it again to my daughter as I drove her to work the next morning. (Polite smile on her part and no assurance on mine that she'd listened to a word of it.) The semester was over, but had I still been teaching, I'm certain I would have regaled my students with this doggy tale—my students being my most reliable depository for stories I want to tell whether or not anyone wants to hear them.

Mired as I had been for the past few years in two separate novels-in-progress, I'd been thinking a lot about the wrong turns, the blind alleys, the mistaken goals that seem so much a part of the long march that is the composition of a novel. So it's possible this little story appealed to me because it's a kind of metaphor for the writing process itself. Not the waking-up-dead part—but the whole up and down the steep hill thing, the trudging toward some recognizable, and then unrecognizable, goal.

Some weeks after reading the story, I heard the novelist John Casey lecture on Aristotle's *Poetics*, and when he mentioned Aristotle's simple, easy-for-you-to-say injunction that every story have a beginning, a middle, and an end, I began to wonder if what had compelled me to repeat this silly little story of the man and his dog was not that deep, sentimental flaw in my own literary sensibilities, but merely the fact that the story itself is a perfect Aristotelian whole with not merely a beginning, middle, and end but pretty damn good ones.

Consider:

A beginning is that which does not itself follow anything by causal necessity, but after which something naturally is or comes to be.

An old man wakes up one morning, calls to his dog, and heads out on a lovely walk down a familiar country road.

As the two go along leisurely, enjoying the scenery and the fine weather, the old man slowly begins to recall that the dog at his side died many years ago, when the old man himself was just leaving his boyhood. Delighted as he is to see his dog again, the man can't help but conclude that if this friend of his youth has returned to him, then he, too, must have died. And indeed, as he walks, the old man remembers his own peaceful passing.

A perfect beginning. Well, maybe not the "An old man wakes up" part. Anyone who has taught fledgling fiction writers knows the bane of those "The alarm clock rang" opening lines—although Kafka and Katherine Anne Porter, to name just two, pull them off pretty well.

What makes this beginning so perfect is the magical moment when the old man, walking *leisurely* along in a familiar landscape with his dog, as—it is implied—is their morning routine, *slowly begins to recall* that the dog has returned to him from a time long past. What a surge of joy is implied in those simple, and amazingly understated, lines—a resurrection, a return of what was lost. A hint of magic.

The storyteller's art is, always, the conjurer's art, and what we look for in beginnings, whether we know it or not, is the first hint of that magic.

For many years, I co-taught a workshop at the Sewanee Writers' Conference with Tony Earley, a brilliant fiction writer and essayist. Once, hoping to illustrate the idea of a reliable or unreliable narrator, Tony told a story from his childhood. On a vacation in the country, his parents, it seemed, wanted some peace and privacy in their cottage one afternoon, as parents of small children are on occasion inclined to do, and so locked the screen door while little Tony was playing outside. As small children of amorous parents are inclined to do, Tony, of course, sensing they wanted him out, demanded to be let in. He rattled the screen door and made various entreaties and was rebuffed by his father each time until little Tony finally got the terrific notion to tell his parents, through the screen, "I saw a snake out here."

This, of course, brought his father outside. As father and son made their search around the property, Tony's father asked him to describe the snake. Delighted by the excellent result of his lie, Tony became increasingly more explicit in his descriptions until he added, "It's got two heads," going immediately, as far as his father was concerned, from reliable to unreliable narrator.

It's as good an illustration of getting the details right as any I've ever heard, but Tony's story also says something about magic. The magic not in little Tony's credulity-straining lie, but the magic in the moment he said, "I saw a snake out here," and his father, in his imagination—and despite more pressing and appealing real-world distractions—saw the snake, too. The magic, the storyteller's magic, is contained in those moments in which both son (the author) and father (the reader) saw that snake out there in their minds' eyes and went about trying to find it. During those moments, until the spell was broken by the wrong detail, the snake *was* there, conjured by the storyteller's words.

Whether we're aware of it or not—and there's no reason for readers to be aware of such things—we look for that magic in every opening of every story, a conjuring of a place, of a voice, of a way of seeing that shows us both the material world of the story and the shimmer of the artist's skill.

Of course, I'm not just talking Harry Potter magic here. Not even magical realism, although Gabriel García Márquez's well-trampled opening paragraph in *One Hundred Years of Solitude* is as good an example as I can think of:

Many years later, as he faced the firing squad, Colonel Aureliano Buendía was to remember that distant afternoon when his father took him to discover ice. At that time Macondo was a village of twenty adobe houses, built on the bank of a river of clear water that ran along a bed of polished stones, which were white and enormous, like prehistoric eggs. The world was so recent that many things lacked names, and in order to indicate them it was necessary to point.

But consider, too, the perhaps less heralded magic of Virginia Woolf's opening paragraphs in *Jacob's Room*:

"So of course," wrote Betty Flanders, pressing her heels rather deeper in the sand, "there was nothing for it but to leave."

Slowly welling from the point of her gold nib, pale blue ink dissolved the full stop; for there her pen stuck; her eyes fixed, and tears slowly filled them. The entire bay quivered; the lighthouse wobbled; and she had the illusion that the mast of Mr. Connor's little yacht was bending like a wax candle in the sun. She winked quickly. Accidents were awful things. She winked again. The mast was straight; the waves were regular; the lighthouse was upright; but the blot had spread.

The magic here being the way the writer, the great prestidigitator, utterly changes the visible world—now you see it, now you don't—by passing it through the transforming prism of Betty Flanders's tears.

And here's Dickens, the great conjurer himself:

My father's family name being Pirrip, and my Christian name Philip, my infant tongue could make of both names nothing longer or more explicit than Pip. So, I called myself Pip, and came to be called Pip.

I give Pirrip as my father's family name, on the authority of his tombstone and my sister—Mrs. Joe Gargery, who married the blacksmith. As I never saw my father or my mother, and never saw any likeness of either of them (for their days were long before the days of photographs), my first fancies regarding what they were like, were unreasonably derived from their tombstones. The shape of the letters on my father's, gave me an odd idea that he was a square, stout, dark man, with curly black hair. From the character and turn of the inscription, *"Also Georgiana Wife of the Above,"* I drew a childish conclusion that my mother was freckled and sickly. To five little stone lozenges, each about a foot and a half long, which were arranged in a neat row beside their grave, and were sacred to the memory of five little brothers of mine—who gave up trying to get a living, exceedingly early in that universal struggle—I am indebted for a belief I religiously entertained that they had all been born on their backs with their hands in their trousers-pockets, and had never taken them out in this state of existence.

Language becomes incantation, and the conjured world is both a real and an imagined place, an authentic *and* an enchanted landscape. The voice in our ear is both a voice we know as well as our own, and one we have never heard before. It shows us the bleak image of the five small graves and, simultaneously, the dear, adorable shape of five children with their hands forever in their trouser pockets.

Inundated as we are by story—internet story and television story and gossip and horror and mass murder everywhere—it is this shimmer of magic that remains the province of the fiction writer alone. A magic that allows us to see, to recognize, what we have never seen before. To marvel at the familiarity of the conjured world even as we glimpse the never-before-seen enchantment of it all.

As the two go along leisurely, enjoying the scenery and the fine weather, the old man slowly begins to recall that the dog at his side

died many years ago, when the old man himself was just leaving
his boyhood . . . And indeed, as he walks, the old man remembers
his own peaceful passing.

A beginning that gives us character, situation, movement forward, and, above all, magic. No wonder it passed the Rufous test.
Middle:

A middle is that which follows something as some other
thing follows it.
"Pets aren't allowed here."

The old man looks at the handsome fellow behind the gate and
the street of gold beyond him. He looks up at the sunlight on the
beautiful arch and down at his dog.

"I'll be going along, then," the old man says, and he turns and
walks back down the hill and out onto the road.

I have a writer friend who calls the point at which she has
reached the middle of a novel-in-progress *middle of book syn-*
drome. "Mobs," she says. "Rhymes with *sobs.*"

The world has been created, the voice established, characters
sent out along their paths. All the creative energy spent on the
initial conjuring, the beginning, all the high hopes the writer
has for the imagined end, now sag a bit, flag a bit, as the middle
of the book approaches.

That simple story-driving engine: *And then what happened?*
And then what happened? becomes, in the middle of a story, a
slightly more impatient, *Now what? Now what?*

And, as the "Animals in Heaven" story shows us, the answer
is: *Now, things change.*

Now, Gatsby's house goes dark, and the parties end.

Now, Emma Bovary returns from the marquis's ball with the

viscount's lovely cigar box in hand, and her boredom suddenly becomes unbearable . . .

Now, Cathy is brought back to Wuthering Heights after her stay with the Lintons, and poor Heathcliff hardly knows her.

Now, Marlow is convinced he will not find Kurtz alive:

For the moment that was the dominant thought. There was a sense of extreme disappointment, as though I had found out I had been striving after something altogether without a substance. I couldn't have been more disgusted if I had travelled all this way for the sole purpose of talking with Mr. Kurtz. Talking with . . . I flung one shoe overboard and became aware that that was exactly what I had been looking forward to—a talk with Kurtz. I made the strange discovery that I had never imagined him as doing, you know, but as discoursing. I didn't say to myself, 'Now I will never see him,' or 'Now I will never shake him by the hand,' but, 'Now I will never hear him.' The man presented himself as a voice. Not of course that I did not connect him with some sort of action. Hadn't I been told in all the tones of jealousy and admiration that he had collected, bartered, swindled, or stolen more ivory than all the other agents together? That was not the point. The point was in his being a gifted creature, and that of all his gifts the one that stood out preeminently, that carried with it a sense of real presence, was his ability to talk, his words—the gift of expression, the bewildering, the illuminating, the most exalted and the most contemptible, the pulsating stream of light, or the deceitful flow from the heart of an impenetrable darkness.

The antidote to "mobs," then, is, quite simply: change. Our narrator becomes aware. (*Now I will never hear him.*) Our protagonists get what they want and then discover it's not what was imagined. They change their minds. Reconsider. Lose heart. Turn away. Continue along on the road, or find another road, climb another steep hill toward another, less certain, goal, despair, resolve, walk on air—to borrow from Seamus Heaney—against their better judgment.

And the end:

> *An end, on the contrary, is that which itself naturally follows some other thing, either by necessity or as a rule, but has nothing following it.*

The satisfaction "Animals in Heaven" provides results, no doubt, from its modest cleverness: a cleverness, we only recognize at the end, that the teller of the tale was aware of all along—from the first words. Had the story begun, "An old man dies one night and finds himself at the pearly gates," our sense of delight at the end of the tale might not be so keen.

But when we reach the end of the story, we can look back at that offhanded and seemingly inadvertent phrase, "calls to his dog"—a phrase that we, naïve, new to the tale, barely notice on first reading—and see now how cleverly it was planted, how cleverly it hid its role as the essential element of the story, for out of it blossoms the old man's realization that he has died, his rejection of the first heaven, the revelation of the nature of the second, authentic one, and, finally, the story's whole reason for being. No dog, no story—no plot, no happy resolution.

We're probably more accustomed to praising the cleverness of jokes and comedy sketches and small children, but it's not a bad element to consider even in the headiest of literary novels and stories. I think of cleverness as that happy satisfaction we feel when we understand that what the novel has revealed to us at its end *the author knew all along*. I don't mean by this a surprise or a piece of information previously withheld—that's the province of stories whose endings leave us feeling deceived, not delighted. Rather, I mean the sense that, from its first sentence, the novel has been, inevitably, heading toward this conclusion.

A good ending also sends us forward, much as a good beginning does, into what Isak Dinesen in her short story "The Blank Page" calls the "silence at the end of the story." (If the storyteller has been true to the story, she says, the silence will speak.) But a good ending also casts a light back through the novel, back to the first chapter and scene and word. Naïve as we were when we first encountered these words, just following along, asking, *And then what happened? And then what happened?*, or, further along, *Now what? Now what?*, on a second reading we can pause to appreciate the author's design. We can appreciate the story's cleverness.

Cleverness, wholeness, an appreciation for design, yes—but a good ending does something more. It says something. It says something about us.

Years and years ago, when I was writing one of my first reviews for the book review section of a major newspaper, I mentioned to the editor that I thought a certain novel was ultimately unsatisfying because it lacked a moral vision. The editor didn't like the term. "I have no moral vision, either," she told me.

I thought of suggesting she might want to make an appointment with a metaphysician, but that was only hours later. *Staircase wit*, as the French say.

Moral vision. The modern reader, and critic, recoil a bit at the phrase—it seems, these days, to portend a scold; it seems to be the province of religious tracts and right-wing politics—but I think it's as much a part of what we look for in the ending of a novel or a story as cleverness, magic, and Aristotle's consistent whole. Put simply: We look for what the novel says that's true for us all. We look for us.

Consider *The Great Gatsby*'s famous ending, "And so we beat on, boats against the current, borne back ceaselessly into the past."

Now hear the difference the slightest pronoun change, the slightest change in perspective, can make:

And so I beat on, a boat against the current, borne back ceaselessly into my past.

And so he beat on, a boat against the current, borne back ceaselessly to his boyhood in St. Paul.

Or, "postmodernly":

And so you beat on, you boat against the current, you, borne back ceaselessly into wherever it was you came from.

The ending of "Animals in Heaven" doesn't try to convince us that loyalty to our friends is good—it simply acknowledges a truth universally known: that loyalty *is* good. But in doing so, it acknowledges that there *are* universal truths to be known, that there are in human experience elemental notions of good (and bad) that we, being human, share. A novel about loyalty— *Billy Budd, Beloved, Great Expectations, The Quiet American, A Gathering of Old Men, The Remains of the Day*—will show us the complexity, drama, rewards, and difficulties of this truth, but the truth, the *we* of it, is there.

Of course, it can be argued that there are no unassailable notions of elemental good. That another version of "Animals in Heaven" might just as well prove that loyalty—to friends, to dead dogs, for instance—is a foolish burden that will result in the loss of wealth and beauty, the kind of wealth and beauty only selfishness can buy. An ending in which an old man is stuck for eternity on an overgrown tract of useless land where he has to pump his own water and endure the company of smug people who read books just because of his blind loyalty to an old dog might also illustrate some universal truth. But not one I'd have felt compelled to share with my dog-walking neighbors or the people I love.

It didn't occur to me, of course, that day on the driveway, that the little Irish story was a bit of Aristotelian perfection. (Although it may have made Rufous—who is of a philosophical bent—feel better about having his walk delayed.) And I'm quite certain that the original author of the story—and I've since learned that versions of this tale appear in a variety of cultures—had no idea of this either. I like to think the story was first conjured for a child who worried about whether pets go to heaven. Or maybe it was told by a loving dog owner who'd been betrayed by a friend. Whatever its origins, it was a good tale, with its nice beginning, middle, and end, and because it was a good tale, whoever first heard it felt compelled to tell it to someone else, who told it to someone else, and so on, right on down to this moment, when I have found my excuse to tell it to you.

SENTENCING

It sometimes happens that immediately after I give a reading—especially if I've read something new and untried, something I've never spoken out loud before—I am at a loss to know: one, if anything I've written has made any sense; two, if the audience has even heard me; and three, if I should burn the manuscript.

I find myself in a kind of stunned perplexity, a pathetic state of cluelessness, anxiety, doubt, and regret that cannot be penetrated by even the kindest, most reassuring response.

I was in just such a state a number of years ago, after a reading I gave at a local university, when, on the way to the reception, I climbed into the car of my host, a poet I much admire, who said, casually, as he leaned over the steering wheel to reach for the ignition, "You sure do love a sentence."

In my altered, post-reading state, I heard "sentence" and assumed "prison sentence."

I heard, "You sure do love your sentence." I heard, "Sentenced to mediocrity, you nevertheless seem to love it." I heard, "What a shame to be imprisoned by your sentences, which make no sense whatsoever, but you seem to be enjoying your terrible incarceration, so go figure."

I heard, "Confined as you are to your delusions of authorship, you sure do love your sentence . . ."

Fortunately, my poet friend was a careful driver, so he didn't turn to see my face blanch and crumble—I'm envisioning here the white cliffs of Dover disintegrating into the sea—before I did a mental version of one of those Looney Tunes, after-the-anvil-falls, jowl-fluttering recoveries and realized he was just being nice.

"Sentenced to sentences," I finally replied.

I'm sure the poet never understood why his kind words so depressed me.

I mention this not to wallow in my insecurities but to spur you, perhaps, to think about sentences.

Not the long sentence—the life sentence—of our desire to write fiction, but that elemental collection of words, the shaping of which constitutes our daily work: the sentence as the pickaxe and hard rock, the metal press and license plate, if you will, of our sentence to literary labor.

And that's enough of that.

Let's start first with first sentences.

It seems to me that a good deal of time is spent in writing workshops talking about first sentences. Which is, I believe, as it should be.

You need only consider how many novels and stories can be identified by their first sentence alone in order to appreciate the importance—the burden and the opportunity—of a first line. Proportionately speaking, I don't know that there's another art form that can be so readily recognized by so small a sample.

(Music lovers are welcome to object, since I hear in my head already the first notes of "Rhapsody in Blue" or *West Side Story* or Beethoven's Fifth.)

- Call me Ishmael.
- Happy families are all alike; every unhappy family is unhappy in its own way.
- Once upon a time and a very good time it was there was a moocow coming down along the road and this moocow that was coming down along the road met a nicens little boy named baby tuckoo . . .
- As Gregor Samsa awoke one morning from uneasy dreams, he found himself transformed in his bed into a gigantic insect.
- Mrs. Dalloway said she would buy the flowers herself.
- I stand here ironing, and what you asked me moves tormented back and forth with the iron.
- Under certain circumstances there are few hours in life more agreeable than the hour dedicated to the ceremony known as afternoon tea.
- In the town there were two mutes, and they were always together.

John McPhee has said that the lead of an article serves as a searchlight that shines down into the body of a piece—which is a good enough description for a work of nonfiction, where story is already formed, has already happened, and needs only to be reported—but the first sentence of a piece of fiction serves as much more than searchlight or hook or even lure to the reluctant reader. The first sentence in a work of fiction places the first limitation on the utterly limitless world of the author's imagination. Before that first sentence is composed, anything is possible. The fiction writer is free to write about anything at all—we are, after all, just making this stuff up—in any voice at all: a child's, a dog's, a dead man's, a god in his heaven, even in the voice of the author herself.

The blank page is nothing less than the wondrous realm of infinite possibilities, and the first words we place on it are nothing less than, well, a sentence, the prison kind, a confinement of all that roving, beautiful, undefined promise into a particular story bound by time and place (four prison walls, a floor, and a ceiling) and voice (of the prisoner, of the other inmates) and rules (our jailor), narrative rules and grammatical rules, rules of logic and composition, experience and sense, rules that we must attend to even if—most particularly if—we set out to break them.

The novelist Gloria Naylor called the first sentence of a piece of fiction the story's DNA, for out of it, she said, arises the second sentence and the third, the fourth—all the way, I would add, to the very last. For if the writer's any good, the first sentence will strike a chord, a tone, a mood, a music that will reverberate throughout the story or the novel, resounding in all kinds of ways through every sentence, all the way to the end.

"Mrs. Dalloway said she would buy the flowers herself" leads us some two hundred pages later to:

> "I will come," said Peter, but he sat on for a moment. What is this terror? What is this ecstasy? he thought to himself. What is it that fills me with extraordinary excitement?
>
> It is Clarissa, he said.
>
> For there she was.

For there she was being the last sentence of the novel whose first sentence begins with *Mrs. Dalloway* and ends with *herself.*

For there she was. Mrs. Dalloway. Herself.

And what possible novel could conclude with the earnest, high-blown language of this singular consciousness:

April 26: Mother is putting my new secondhand clothes in order. She prays now, she says, that I may learn in my own life and away from home and friends what the heart is and what it feels. Amen. So be it. Welcome, O life! I go to encounter for the millionth time the reality of experience and to forge in the smithy of my soul the uncreated conscience of my race.

April 27: Old father, old artificer, stand me now and ever in good stead.

A conclusion the novel could not have reached if it had not begun by staking its claim to language, to perspective, to its own music in a first line such as:

Once upon a time and a very good time it was there was a moocow coming down along the road and this moocow that was coming down the road met a nicens little boy named baby tuckoo . . .

Perspective—first person, third person, limited, omniscient—voice, rhythm, character, subject, and, yes, story all begin to be established, memorably or not, in the first sentence.

No wonder we spend some time in fiction-writing workshops talking about first sentences.

And yet, in spite of all that conversation, I can offer you no formula for what makes a first sentence a good first sentence. And I'd be suspicious of anyone who claims to have one. But here's something I have learned: more often than not, the first sentence in the draft of the story under consideration in a writing workshop is not the best sentence to begin with.

In fact, more often than not, the simple request that workshop readers look through a given piece and find a better first sentence results in all kinds of marvelous choices, many of them found on page 2, or on page 15, or even somewhere in the last paragraph.

Why is this?

For the novice fiction writer, it's often just a case of holding back, holding on to the good stuff, the good writing, the fine detail, the authentic voice—the very thing that first drove the writer to the blank page—until the reader has paid his dues or demonstrated her devotion by wading through the meandering descriptions or the flat dialogue or the tedious philosophies the writer is determined to unload at the start.

We writers are all—let's face it—lonely souls with mountainous egos as delicate as white cliffs of baby powder, and we all harbor the belief that any reader who dares to ask, a mere twenty pages in, "Why should I care about this?" or "What are you talking about?" is a reader clearly unworthy of our gifts.

(I recently witnessed this phenomenon—call it the insecure writer's mask of disdain—at a crowded literary festival, where the young author of a celebrated first novel was asked by a reader, an older woman, if the confusion she felt at the beginning of his book, trying to keep all of his characters straight, was somehow what he intended the reader to feel. After an uncomfortable moment of frigid silence, the author coolly replied, "I think your confusion says more about you as a reader than it does about me as a writer." Humiliating the questioner, insulting the audience—made up mostly of older women—and demonstrating to all that precocious literary talent yields no immunity from being a jerk.)

Tedious openings may well be an author's way of gauging a reader's unquestioning devotion, but more often, I think, the novice holds back out of fear that if he gets right to it, right to the good part—to the thing that drove him to the blank page to begin with—then the novel will die in paragraph two, perhaps even sentence two, because there's nothing more to say.

But first sentences also fail when the novice, or the not-so-novice, begins the story or the novel with an overdetermined plan—a plot outline with Roman numerals, large caps and small caps, or a detailed synopsis that accounts for every connection and every turn—so that the first written sentence of the actual piece has no more energy, no more music, than line one of a daily to-do list.

To paraphrase Henry James, such a writer begins by merely filling out a form, and so the language of the first line—the story's DNA—is serviceable at best, lackadaisical at worst. It sounds shopworn because it is shopworn—it has been handled over and over again in the author's mind—even if it is fresh to the page.

In my experience, those far superior first sentences buried on page 2 or 7 or 18 of a work-in-progress are sentences that have appeared without pre-planning, sentences written according to no formula, no scheme—sentences that are formed not in moments of determined inspiration or the huffing pursuit of brilliance, but in the pen-to-paper, fingers-to-the-keyboard (pickaxe-to-hardrock?) daily work of getting a story told. The kind of sentence that surprises and delights even the writer herself when it is called to her attention as a possible, a preferable, beginning.

When I consider those memorable first lines in literature, from Tolstoy's to Tillie Olsen's, the single thing they all seem to have in common is authority—a word, in this context, perhaps easier to define by what it is not than by precisely what it is.

Call me Ishmael, for instance, is not, *I suppose you could say I've gone by a lot of different names in my life, after all, I was a small, shy kid, and I was picked on a lot, but out of all the names and nicknames I've had over the course of my twenty-five years,*

I'd probably prefer that you refer to me by the one that you might think sounds somewhat old-fashioned or even, I don't know, kind of biblical, like my mother was some kind of Evangelical or something, which she wasn't, she was agnostic, although she did read the Bible when she couldn't find anything else to read . . .

If there is an unwritten preamble to *Call me Ishmael*, it is something like *Sit down, shut up, listen.*

Authority. What all these memorable first sentences convey, in all their variety, is confidence. No equivocation. No building up to the good stuff.

Listen, they say. I have a story to tell. I know how to tell it. Trust me.

- It is a truth universally acknowledged, that a single man in possession of a good fortune must be in want of a wife.
- In my younger and more vulnerable years my father gave me some advice that I've been turning over in my mind ever since.
- My mother died today.
- 124 was spiteful. Full of a baby's venom.
- Long ago in 1945 all the nice people in England were poor, allowing for exceptions.

We can't always, or even often, bring that authority and confidence to the first sentences we write—that first sentence meant to pin down, confine, limit, arrest the infinite possibilities of everything not yet written—but we can often come across it after we've begun, after the story has begun to take shape, to warm up, if you will. Sentences that appear as our voice finds itself, as we lose our self-consciousness or our plan, as we, inadvertently, just stumbling along, find the far better sentence with which to begin—on page 10, page 20, page 106.

The key word here is, perhaps, *inadvertently*.

I once had a conversation with an editor about Cormac McCarthy's work. This editor was both a poet and a novelist himself, as well as an excellent translator, a brilliant, even famous, man of letters. At the time, he had not read any of McCarthy's novels, and he asked me what I thought of them. I replied that I sometimes found his plots and characters a bit too heavy on Manly Men, but, I said, his sentences are beautiful.

The editor moaned. "Oh, God," he said. "Spare me the beautiful sentences."

I don't agree—I love a beautiful sentence the way I love a good caramel or a mellow Brunello—something fine to linger over, to savor—but I do see his point. In my years of writing and teaching, I've often seen how the straining after beautiful sentences can ruin many a promising first draft—my own and others'.

No doubt it has something to do with self-consciousness, the same self-consciousness that can sink an opening line. The very intention to craft a beautiful sentence may be precisely the thing that guarantees you'll write a clunker, perhaps because a beautiful sentence requires—maybe all beauty does—something of the inadvert, the unintentional, the spontaneous.

Eudora Welty said, "Beauty is not a means, not a way of furthering a thing in the world. It is a result; it belongs to ordering, to form, to aftereffect."

And yet, especially for those of us of the literary persuasion, the temptation to craft beautiful sentences, to discover look-at-me phrases, is strong. After all, reviewers seem to love them—if only because, I sometimes suspect, citing beautiful sentences in a book review involves no discussion of meaning, no risky interpretation of theme, is only a matter of saying,

"Hey, take a gander at these pretty lines," and then easily filling up the assignment's word count with a string of quotations.

Here's a reviewer praising C. E. Morgan's excellent first novel, *All the Living*:

> There are remarkable sentences on almost every page: "The white bunched blossoms had breasted out of their buds overnight"; a trailer "jagged out like an aluminum finger from a limestone wall topped by firs, bone out of bone."

The reviewer himself perhaps not noticing, in his fervor to compile a list, that it seems more contradiction than proof of his praise that the first two examples share similar constructions: blossoms that breasted out and trailers that jutted out . . . bone out of bone.

And here's the critic James Wood citing some favorite phrases from Emma Cline's novel *The Girls*:

> On every other page, it seems, there is something remarkable—an immaculate phrase, a boldly modifying adverb, a metaphor or simile that makes a sudden, electric connection between its poles . . . she evokes for us with sunlit clarity every detail and texture of her California childhood: "the secret flash of other driveways, other lives," as seen from a car; "the nothing jump of soda in my throat" (is anyone likely to better that?); the "rotted pucker" of sherry, on first taste; Evie's mother at a party, her "neck getting blotchy with nerves"; the shy way that she "looked at herself in the oracle of the mirror"; "the sparkly mess of flies I'd swept from the corners."

It strikes me that Wood, too, might have gotten his critic's needle stuck when composing this list: *secret flash, nothing jump, rotted pucker, sparkly mess . . .*

He offers another such list in his review of Lauren Groff's
Fates and Furies:

> Groff's unbracketed language . . . is thrillingly good—precise,
> lyrical, rich, both worldly and epically transfiguring. Young
> Lotto, seen cycling from a distance, is a "mantis on his bicycle";
> a dog's erection is "a tube of lipstick all the way extended." The
> sound of a swimming pool—"the pool suckled at its gutters."
> A lake is "poxed by the touch of scattered rain." A bus, lower-
> ing itself to let people down, "knelt the passengers off like a
> carnival elephant." Bubbles "flea-jump" out of the top of a
> champagne glass. There are many more examples, on page after
> page. The prose is beautiful and vigorously alert . . .

It should perhaps serve as word to the wise—and to any of us
who labor too hard to achieve attention-getting, "beautiful"
phrases—that Wood ultimately finds both novels lacking. In the
case of *The Girls*, in fact, he pans the very form of the sentences
he at first seems to praise:

> The sentence fragment is suddenly everywhere in fiction
> today, and increasingly seems an emblematic unit of the
> literary age. It is vivid and provisional, inhabits the vital mo-
> ment, and renders the world in a cascade of tiled perceptions.
> But it also tends to restrict a novel's ability to make larger
> connections, larger coherences, the expansion and deepening
> of its themes. The form of a novel is the accumulation of its
> sentences; in this case, the tempo of the sentence becomes
> the stammering tempo of the form . . .

It may also be beneficial to recall that even in these matters of sentences, beauty can be in the eye of the beholder.

Across many decades, I read, "the pool suckled at its gutters," and hear a poetry professor, a man ever on guard for pathetic fallacies, call out to us scribbling undergrads: *Who* is suckling *what*?

Further proof, too, of something I've always suspected: that a fiction writer can learn nothing useful at all from reading the work of book critics.

We might, however, learn something from the poets. Consider the way the poet Gwendolyn Brooks in her brief and brilliant novel *Maud Martha* makes music of her sentences with alliteration and repetition, as well as solid visual images that nevertheless *swish* by:

> The name "New York" glittered in front of her like the silver in the shops on Michigan Boulevard. It was silver, and it was solid, and it was remote: it was behind glass, it was behind bright glass like the silver in the shops. It was not for her. Yet.
>
> When she was out walking, and with grating iron swish a train whipped by, off, above, its passengers were always, for her comfort, New York bound. She sat inside with them. She leaned back in the plush. She sped, past farms, through tiny towns, where people slept, kissed, quarreled, ate midnight snacks; unfortunate folks who were not New York bound and never would be.

Or consider the powerful simplicity of these sentences from Seamus Heaney's translation of *Beowulf*:

> In off the moors, down through the mist bands
> God-cursed Grendel came greedily loping.
> The bane of the race of men roamed forth,
>   hunting for a prey in the high hall.

Under the cloud-murk he moved towards it
   until it shone above him, a sheer keep
   of fortified gold . . .
Spurned and joyless, he journeyed on ahead
   and arrived at the bawn. The iron-braced door
Turned on its hinge when his hands touched it.
Then his rage boiled over, he ripped open
The mouth of the building, maddening for blood,
   pacing the length of the patterned floor
With his loathsome tread, while a baleful light,
Flame more than light, flared from his eyes.

No linguistic somersaults or headstands here, only gorgeous clarity.

Of course, whenever I think of beautiful sentences—sentences worth savoring, turning over again and again in your reading mind—I think of Nabokov. And among the many superb examples his work provides, I love this single chapter from his novel *Bend Sinister*:

Holding your cupped hands together, dear, and progressing with the cautious and tremulous steps of tremendous age (although hardly fifteen) you crossed the porch; stopped; gently worked open the glass door by means of your elbow; made your way past the caparisoned grand piano, traversed the sequence of cool carnation-scented rooms, found your aunt in the *chambre violette*—

I think I want to have the whole scene repeated. Yes, from the beginning. As you came up the stone steps of the porch, your eyes never left your cupped hands, the pink chink between the two thumbs. Oh, what were you carrying? Come on now. You wore a striped (dingy white and pale blue) sleeveless jersey, a dark-blue girl-scout skirt, untidy orphan-black stockings and a pair of old chlorophyl-stained tennis shoes. Between the pillars of the porch geometrical sunlight touched your reddish brown bobbed hair, your plump neck and the vaccination mark on your sunburned arm. You moved slowly through a cool and sonorous drawing room, then entered a room where the carpet and armchairs and curtains were purple and blue. From various mirrors your cupped hands and lowered head came towards you and your movements were mimicked behind your back. Your aunt, a lay figure, was writing a letter.

"Look," you said.

Very slowly, rosewise, you opened your hands. There, clinging with all its six fluffy feet to the ball of your thumb, the tip of its mouse-grey body slightly excurved, its short, red, blue-ocellated inferior wings oddly protruding forward from beneath the sloping superior ones which were long and marbled and deeply notched—

I think I shall have you go through your act a third time, but in reverse, carrying that hawk moth into the orchard where you found it.

As you went the way you had come (now with the palm of your hand open), the sun that had been lying in state on the parquetry of the drawing-room and on the flat tiger (spread-eagled and bright-eyed beside the piano), leapt at you, climbed the dingy soft rungs of your jersey and struck you right in the face so that all could see (crowding, tier upon tier, in the sky, jostling one another, pointing, feasting their eyes on the young *radabarbára*) its high color and fiery freckles, and the hot cheeks as red as the hind wings basally, for the moth was still clinging to your hand and you were still looking at it as you progressed towards the garden, where you gently transferred it to the lush grass at the foot of an apple tree far from the beady eyes of your little sister.

Where was I at the time? An eighteen-year-old student sitting with a book (*Les Pensées*, I imagine) on a station bench miles away, not knowing you, not known to you. Presently I shut the book and took what was called an omnibus train to the country place where young Hedron was spending the summer. This was a cluster of rentable cottages on a hillside overlooking the river, the opposite bank of which revealed in terms of fir trees and alder bushes the heavily timbered acres of your aunt's estate.

We shall now have somebody else arrive from nowhere— *à pas de loup*, a tall boy with a little black moustache and other signs of hot uncomfortable puberty. Not I, not Hedron. That summer we did nothing but play chess. The boy was your cousin, and while my comrade and I, across the river, pored over Tarrash's collection of annotated games, he would drive you to tears during meals by some intricate and maddening piece of teasing and then, under the pretense of reconciliation, would steal after you into some attic where you were hiding your frantic sobbing, and there would kiss your wet eyes, and hot neck, and tumbled hair and try to get at your armpits and garters for you were a remarkably big ripe girl for your age; but he, in spite of his fine looks and hungry hard limbs, died of consumption a year later.

And still later, when you were twenty and I twenty-three, we met at a Christmas party and discovered that we had been neighbors that summer, five years before—five years lost! And at the precise moment when in awed surprise (awed by the bungling of destiny) you put your hand to your mouth and looked at me with very round eyes and muttered: "But that's where *I* lived!"—I recalled in a flash a green lane near an orchard and a sturdy young girl carefully carrying a lost fluffy nestling, but whether it had been really you no amount of probing and poking could either confirm or disprove.

Fragment from a letter addressed to a dead woman in heaven by her husband in his cups.

These are sentences that don't cry out to be bathed in the reviewer's yellow highlighter—that don't beg for attention by shouting, Look at me, look how cleverly I've put this. Nabokov's sentences compel us to look not at the author's brilliance, but at the emotions evoked—joy, astonishment, regret, grief—the scene, the frame of mind; they ask us not to be moved to admiration for the author, but to be moved by the experience, the shared sensations, the precision of the words. "Very slowly, rosewise, you opened your hands."

Beauty that is not imposed on the sentence but inherent in it—beauty of order, of form, of precise detail, of aftereffect.

And thinking of Nabokov reminds me of another risk we run when we strain too self-consciously after beauty, sentence by sentence: sooner or later, our prose has to get back to the everyday work of the narrative. Soaring rhetoric, poetic observations, highly clever turns of phrase can become utterly exhausting to maintain. You never want to send one sentence so high into the aesthetic stratosphere that the next one—meant only to achieve some mundane task—falls on its face.

Here's the master describing this very struggle for an old, aspiring writer in his story "Lips to Lips":

His leanings were strictly lyrical, descriptions of nature and emotions came to him with surprising facility, but on the other hand he had a lot of trouble with routine items, such as, for instance, the opening and closing of doors, or shaking hands when there were numerous characters in a room, and one person or two persons saluted many people. Furthermore Ilya Borisovich tussled constantly with pronouns, as for example "she," which had a teasing way of referring not only to the heroine but also to her mother or sister in the same sentence, so that in order to avoid repeating a proper name one was often compelled to put "that lady" or "her interlocutress" although no interlocution was taking place.

If you find yourself struggling with transitions between soaring lyricism and sentences that get your character's shoelaces tied, if you find yourself writing sentence after sentence that can only be followed by the sacred hush of a space break—something like the last line of dialogue before the commercial in a soap opera—then perhaps your sentences are trying too hard to be beautiful.

Maybe it's time to aim for sentences that are simply *better*.

But how to achieve even this modest goal?

Well, there's always Strunk and White. There's "Omit needless words," for example. E. B. White's injunction is still a good one. Culling the fat from our prose, the excessive, the unnecessary, is always a helpful exercise, sometimes encouraged by setting yourself the simple task of honing your word count: if your story is 3,556 words long, try cutting it down to 3,400, just to see what happens.

In the last century, when I published my first novel, lady copy editors still roamed the hushed hallways of publishing houses. They did indeed wear cardigans and soft-soled shoes, and they kept their reading glasses on chains around their necks.

These women knew their grammar, of course—my God, they knew their grammar—and they could fact-check the hell out of even the most benign detail or flight of fancy—and these were pre-computer days—but they were also famous for discovering redundancies.

"You used the word 'oval' on page 4," they might query in the margin of a manuscript, in their fine, blue-penciled print. "Do you want to use it again here?"—here being page 76 or 212. Or they would write, "Repetition intentional?" if they found a phrase or an image that reappeared in your work—even at the distance of two hundred pages.

They were relentless, and every writer I met in those days resented them.

But surely this long-suffering and now nearly extinct species made me think about my sentences, my grammar, my vocabulary, my word choice. They forced me to make the case for a repetition I intended and to eliminate those I did not. That blue-penciled margin question—*"Intentional?"*—is, after all, a moment of truth. No matter what you were thinking when you composed the sentence, whether you threw in the repeated word or phrase accidentally or with great thematic purpose, now, in the cool light of the editing process, do you know why it's there?

If you choose the *"It's my book; I am the writer"* defense, do you know what kind of writer you are?

In his translation, with Larissa Volokhonsky, of *Notes from the Underground*, Richard Pevear writes in his preface:

> Repetition is of essence here. When the underground man speaks of consciousness and heightened consciousness, it is always the same word: "consciousness," not "intellectual activity," as one translator has it, not "awareness" as another offers, and never some mixture of the three. The editorial precept of avoiding repetitions, of gracefully varying one's vocabulary, cannot be applied to this writer. His writing is emphatic, heavy-handed, rude.

In the pursuit of better sentences, be your own annoying copy editor, sans eyeglass chain: snip a redundant phrase here, a nonessential clause there. Consider and reconsider your word choice, your refrains. If you're breaking the rules, choosing, perhaps, redundancy over graceful variations, know why.

Also watch out for misplaced modifiers: "Spurned and joyless, *he* journeyed on ahead and arrived at the bawn," not "Spurned and joyless, the bawn awaited him," or "Holding your cupped hands together, dear, and progressing with the cautious and tremulous steps of tremendous age (fifteen!), *you* crossed the porch . . . ," not "*I imagine* how you crossed the porch . . ."

And be careful of semicolons run amok. A sentence with two independent clauses linked by a coordinating conjunction—*and, but, for, or, so, yet*—gets a comma: *In the town there were two mutes, and they were always together.*

No coordinating conjunction, a semicolon: *Happy families are all alike; every unhappy family is unhappy in its own way.*

And check that your verbs aren't burdened by unnecessary *had*s and *would*s.

The past perfect is, of course, a handy tool—especially in establishing background or flashback—but you'll want to return to the simple past as soon as you can, or your sentences may begin tripping up over their *had*s and their *had had*s.

Here's Alice Munro doing a bit of expository flashback in the second section of her story "Trespasses":

This was the year after Harry had quit his job on a newsmag-azine because he was burned out. He had bought the weekly newspaper in this small town, which he remembered from his childhood. His family used to have a summer place on one of the little lakes around here, and he remembered drinking his first beer in the hotel on the main street. He and Eileen and Lauren went there for dinner on their first Sunday night in town.

But the bar was closed. Harry and Eileen had to drink water.

Munro uses the past perfect twice to ensure that the reader understands the transition in time after the first space break—*had quit / had bought*—but she then drops it for the more immediate simple past as soon as the scene of the flashback begins: "He and Eileen and Lauren went there for dinner on their first Sunday night in town."

She would not have been mistaken to write: "He and Eileen and Lauren had gone there for dinner"—the story is still in flashback mode, and so past perfect still applies—but the quick return to simple past allows her to keep the *had*s from clunking up her sentences, and thus she avoids having to write: "But the bar had been closed. Harry and Eileen had had to drink water."

And get the *would*s out, too, when you can, for *would*, indicating a repetition in the past, is also a word that, if left to linger, will clog up the flow of a sentence—a logjam, so to speak—as well as a scene. Handy as it is in describing a routine over time, it is, like the past perfect, a construction best exchanged for simple past as soon as clarity allows.

Consider Katherine Anne Porter in *Noon Wine*:

The years passed, and Mr. Helton never got ready to talk. After his work was finished for the day, he would come up from the barn or the milk house or the chicken house, swinging his lantern, his big shoes clumping like pony hoofs on the hard path. They, sitting in the kitchen in the winter, or on the back porch in summer, would hear him drag out his wooden chair, hear the creak of it tilted back, and then for a little while he would play his single tune on one or another of his harmonicas. The harmonicas were in different keys, some lower and sweeter than the others, but the same changeless tune *went* on [not *would go on*], a strange tune with sudden turns in it, night after night, and sometimes even in the afternoons when Mr. Helton *sat* down [not *would sit* down] to catch his breath. At first the Thompsons liked it very much, and always *stopped* to listen [not *would always stop*]. Later there came a time when they were fairly sick of it and began to wish to each other that he would learn another . . . [most certainly not "they *would* become fairly sick of it and *would* wish he *would* learn another . . .]

Remember, too, that the *would always* verb form carries with it a certain removal from experience as it is lived, and so, if not used judiciously, it can dilute the readers' experience. None of us, when you think about it, lives in the *would always*; we can only see it at a distance. We live in the right now; the *would always* comes later.

And while you're picking off your excess *had*s and *would*s, keep in mind another Strunk and White injunction: "Vary sentence structure." Be aware of the hypnotic vortex of subject-verb, subject-verb, subject-verb—although be careful of, or at least conscious of, using lots of sentence fragments as a cure. Lest you bring down the scorn of book reviewers. Sound fragmented. With limited attention span. Kind of blinky.

Heed well, as well (repetition intentional), Strunk and White's advice to avoid the passive voice. A strong sentence loves a subject. Compare "No crime was committed" to "I am not a crook."

Of course, we've all been taught that most sentences are

strengthened, made lean and more meaningful, by the elimination of adjectives and adverbs . . . but don't overdo this.

My friend Roger Rosenblatt so convinced his writing students that they should banish adjectives from their work that one of them sent him this poem:

> Roses are red
> Violets are blue
> But for Roger
> Just roses and violets will do.

As Gregor Samsa awoke one morning from uneasy dreams, he found himself transformed in his bed into a gigantic insect is not a sentence improved by the elimination of its adjectives. Consider: *As Gregor Samsa awoke one morning from his dreams, he found himself transformed in his bed into an insect*, and you'll understand what is gained by "uneasy" and "gigantic."

Eliminate "tormented" from *I stand here ironing, and what you asked me moves tormented back and forth with the iron*, and you have a first line far less memorable than Olsen's.

E. B. White himself, in answer to a reader of *The Elements of Style*, added a coda to his "Omit needless words" rule:

> It comes down to the meaning of "needless." Often a word can be removed without destroying the structure of a sentence, but that does not necessarily mean that the word is needless or that the sentence has gained by its removal.
>
> If you were to put a narrow construction on the word "needless," you would have to remove thousands of words from Shakespeare, who seldom said anything in six words that could be said in twenty.
>
> Writing is not an exercise in excision; it's a journey into

sound. How about "tomorrow and tomorrow and tomorrow"? One "tomorrow" would suffice, but it's the other two that have made the thing immortal.

A journey into sound: "the sequence of cool carnation-scented rooms" . . . "a strange tune with sudden turns in it."

This is where I might suggest that you read your sentences out loud in order to discover your own sound: the rhythm, pattern, refrain, reprise of your prose.

It's not a bad suggestion at all.

But since I don't do this myself—except when giving a public reading, and I've already mentioned what that particular exercise does for me—I'm sheepish about offering it as advice.

And I worry about self-consciousness.

There's a story that Eudora Welty tells in her interview in *The Paris Review*—about how W. C. Fields, after being shown a detailed analysis of his juggling technique, was not able to juggle again for six years. As far as Fields was concerned, Welty says, all he did was throw some balls up into the air and catch them. Once he thought too much about it, he was a goner.

I once saw the late Elie Wiesel field a number of technical questions from novice writers: Do you know the whole story before you begin the novel? Do you rewrite as you go along? Do you do a lot of research? He answered them all patiently, but in the end, he threw up his hands. "No one knows how a novel gets written," he cried. "It is a mystery."

Workshop feedback and lectures and book reviews, even manuals about the elements of style, can engender a self-consciousness in us that leaves no room for that mystery. A self-consciousness that can stifle both the inadvertent and the innovative, the bit of stumbled-upon magic, the voice never before tried, the beauty that appears only as aftereffect.

Here's the dilemma: We know our stories are unique, uniquely ours, because the lives we have lived that have led us to these stories, to the very words with which we tell them, will never be duplicated. And yet we work out of a literary tradition that has been formed by thousands and thousands of stories not our own, told in voices not our own, the very stories we study and emulate and love.

Delicate egotists that we are, we want to be a part of the tradition that has brought us to the blank page, but we also want to expand it, upend it, make it new. We are all in some way rebellious third graders at heart, and we want the freedom to do as we please—if Dostoevsky can be "emphatic, heavy-handed, rude," why can't I? If old Jimmy Joyce can write those run-ons, why can't I?

When my son was beginning to play the piano seriously, he resolved to study only jazz, to excel at jazz improvisation, jazz composition. I advised him that he might learn more at his tender age—he was eleven or so—if he stuck with playing classical music.

"Do you want to stick with reading the novels other people have written?" he asked me. "Or do you want to write your own?"

All of us who write want to write *our own*.

We want the freedom to do so, to compose and to improvise, and yet we also want some rules, rules of grammar and punctuation, of composition, of logic—both the narrative and the emotional kind. We want to make sense, but we don't want to sound like everyone else. We want to work at our sentences with clear intention, and yet we don't want to refuse the inadvertent. We want to be in control of our nouns and verbs, our repetitions and refrains, and yet we don't want self-consciousness to blot out the mystery of composition.

No wonder it often feels like a sentence—a prison sentence—this working at words in order to add to, and also to surpass, the tradition that first brought us to this effort. It's a longing to be fettered and unfettered at the same time.

My jazz-playing son (yes, he won *that* argument) recently recommended I read *Murray Talks Music*, a collection of interviews with the essayist and critic Albert Murray, one of the founders of Jazz at Lincoln Center.

I've already overdone the whole prison-sentence thing, so I won't strain to draw a connection between what Murray has to say about the blues and our own woeful jailhouse experience working at words—but I love this point he makes:

> That's a very big fallacy in dealing with art. You see, art is a matter of mastering the devices of expression. Just because you suffer doesn't make you an artist. It's the mastery of the means of expression that makes you an artist. People say, well, Bessie Smith sang the blues because she suffered this or that. Why is she always suffering in the twelve-bar chorus? You know what I mean? Twelve-bar chorus, eight-bar chorus, four bars . . .
>
> Art is about form. Art is about *elegant form* . . . and the artist is the first to know when a form is no longer as serviceable as it was. You see? *And that's what innovation is about.* He's trying to keep that form going and he finds it necessary to extend, elaborate it, and refine it; to adjust it to new situations. That's what innovation is about. It's not to get rid of something simply to be getting rid of it, or to turn something around. It's to *continue* something that's indispensable.

We write our own stories in order to continue something that's indispensable.

Not such a bad sentence, after all.

WHAT ABOUT THE BABY?

(For Sue Wheeler)

Here are a few passages I culled from my casual reading of contemporary literary fiction during the first decade of the twenty-first century.
From a highly praised first novel:

You have never seen someone weep until you have witnessed a mother at the funeral of her murdered child. The girl was nine years old. She was removed at night from an open window. It was all over the papers. First she was missing . . . Three days later she was found in an empty lot wrapped in plastic sheeting.

From an acclaimed debut collection of short stories:

Last spring, Samantha Mealey, a nine-year-old girl from your elementary school, was found naked in a maple tree on the public golf course, a length of clothesline around her neck. In fact, you'd met her at the bus stop just a few weeks before she died. She'd been a brassy, fearless little girl with a raucous laugh. On that afternoon, much to the chagrin of her older brother, she'd been trying to pull some boy's pants down and cussing out loud for fun. She was an exciting girl.

You have not had your first kiss, but you are already worried about sex. Just two grades ahead of you, kids are having it already. When you learned that the man who killed Samantha Mealey had raped her before he tied the noose around her neck, what occurred to you was this: At least she didn't die a virgin—a thought you cannot share with even your wickedest friends.

And from another celebrated debut collection:

. . . and finally I had to get my hand around her neck and squeeze a little bit, just enough to settle her down . . . Her face turned as red as a raspberry, and her eyes flipped back in her head till only the whites were showing, and I let up on her and pushed her nose down in the gravel. I remember a mud dauber landed close to her ear, and I smashed it against the side of her head with my hand. She got easy after that, and I got my bibs down and slipped inside her . . .

I clenched both hands around her neck, and this time I didn't let up until there wasn't anything left but her sweet face all bloomed out like a purple flower and a skinny little body turned to wax.

And one more (with apologies), a scene from a story by one of our most prolific literary artists:

Hadley didn't want her agitated visitor to sense how frightened she was of him. Her mistake was in turning away to lead him to the door. Insulting him. He looped an arm around her neck, and in an instant they were struggling off balance. He

grabbed at her, and kissed her—kissed and bit at her lips, like a
suddenly ravenous rodent. Both their wineglasses went flying,
clattering to the floor.

She was trying to draw breath to scream but he'd pushed
her down. She thought he was trying to strangle her, then it
seemed that he was still kissing her, or trying to. Panicked, she
jammed her elbows into his chest, his ribs; his mouth closed
over hers and she thought that he would bite off her lip. With
a kind of manic elation, he was murmuring what sounded like
You like me! You want this! Grunting with effort, he straddled
her, his face flushed with emotion; their struggle had become
purely physical, and urgent, enacted now in near-silence, except
for their panting.

I suppose it can be argued that in literature, as in life, if
you go looking for a trend, you're more than likely to find it.
The novelist R.H.W. Dillard has a theory regarding chickens in
film, something along the lines that if you look for a chicken
somewhere in the background or the foreground of every movie,
you'll see one.

A few years ago, my graduate fiction class at Johns Hopkins,
hoping to unlock the secret of one kind of literary success, noticed that a strange majority of the stories published in *The New
Yorker* that semester featured auto mechanics or repair shops—
indication, surely, of nothing more than someone on staff with
car problems.

I can't say that in my casual reading of literary fiction
during these years I'd gone looking for dead little girls or rape
scenes. I don't claim either to be so widely read in contemporary fiction to conclude that this odd collection of disturbing—
dare I say offensive (yeah, I'm the mother of a daughter; I'll say

offensive)—and often (worse yet) gratuitous scenes of violence against women and girls represented anything but an odd if wearying coincidence.

For all I know, there may have been an equal number of stories and novels featuring skinned and strangled Labrador retrievers or the lifeless, degraded, naked bodies of precocious little boys.

My casual reading habits are just that. I spend the vast majority of my reading time with student work, or galleys that arrive on my doorstep, or rereading the books I'm teaching or the authors who lured me into this profession in the first place, and in the time that's left over, I tend to pick up whatever's at hand or what someone has lent me or something my students or book club friends are reading. Which pretty much describes the route by which I stumbled across these passages. Coincidence, surely. Bad luck, perhaps.

Or maybe it's just art imitating television: no one who watched dramatic television in those years, or even just the shows' promos, could have avoided coming to the conclusion that nothing makes for better drama than the naked body of a murdered young woman. As a TV critic wrote at the time, there are far more serial killers in popular entertainment than there have ever been in real life. Perhaps in my casual reading in those years, I'd just come upon a lot of writers who were watching too much TV.

Or maybe it was an economics thing, some weird, literary equivalent of the reality that a downturn in the economy sparks an upturn in acts of domestic violence—that is, violence against women. Even in the stories we tell.

Or maybe somehow in the first decade of the twenty-first century—what with 9/11, the Iraq War, the recession—contemporary readers, and nonreaders, had reached the state that Nathanael West attributes to his hero in *Miss Lonelyhearts*:

Like a dead man, only friction could make him warm or violence make him mobile.

Whatever the cause and effect, whatever the unhappy happenstance that brought these scenes into my reading life at the
time, I decided late one night that I'd had enough. Lying in
bed, looking for something to worry about before sleep came
and finding nothing more fertile than the state of contemporary fiction—kids were okay, husband was busy, mother was
well, colleagues were genial, novel was moving along, eco-
nomic catastrophe had been avoided, and, surely, someday, the
war would end—I resolved to take a hiatus from reading rape
scenes or descriptions of the dead bodies of women and girls,
no matter how brilliant the author or apparently essential the
plot twist.

I knew immediately that my resolution would mean that I'd
have to miss—for now, at least—the book everyone was talking
about, Roberto Bolaño's *2666*, with its three hundred pages that
tally, as one review put it, "the bodies of women and girls who
have run out of time . . . Bodies . . . stabbed or strangled or shot
or burned, often raped in multiple places, sometimes mutilated;
found on desert roads or school grounds, in alleys and hills and
a dump . . ." Given the length of the novel, it was probably going
to be a long while before I got to it anyway.

As a woman who reads, I've taken such self-imposed exiles
before. I was in graduate school when I came across a story by a
famous writer, a writer I admired, in a friend's copy of *Playboy*,
and by the time I got to the lovely and lyrical description of
our hero's change of heart regarding his blond bimbo girlfriend
who had passed out in the theater because her clothes were too
tight but whose slack-jawed unconsciousness struck him, finally,
as so much more worthy of his love than her dumb, waking self,

I vowed to take a hiatus from this writer's work, no matter his stellar reputation or how much I could learn from him.

And just about the time I relented—his sentences are so good—and readmitted this author into my reading life, I came upon another story, also by a male writer I greatly admired, that featured a woman who sleeps solidly through most of her time on earth (she even remains in bed while her child is rushed to the hospital) and, as a result, is much beloved by her wakeful husband. Which reminded me as well of the García Márquez story "Sleeping Beauty and the Airplane," which is about a man who falls in love with his sleeping seatmate. Trends are, as I say, where you look for them—although, as a woman who reads, I'll take beloved and unconscious over raped and murdered, if those are the only two choices.

Anyway, with nothing better to worry about that night, I vowed to stop reading rape scenes, to close the book, no matter its author, whenever I stumbled upon a dead little girl or a mutilated woman.

Of course, as soon as I made the resolution, I began to reprimand myself for my intolerance, for my prudishness, my creaking feminism, my Catholic Legion of Decency censorship, my motherly high dudgeon. "I find the material offensive" is not, I was well aware, an intelligent response to a work of art—even when it is, alas, the most authentic response one can muster.

Lying awake, I somewhat sheepishly recalled a friend who once volunteered to lead a film discussion for a group of senior citizens, all women. Her first selection for the group was the movie *Julia*, based on Lillian Hellman's memoir *Pentimento*—a wonderful choice, it seemed, one that would surely get the women talking about their own early careers or love affairs or, certainly, their own experiences as young women during the Second World

War. Anticipating their enthusiasm for the film, my friend even gave out copies of Hellman's book before the movie started.

As you'll remember, Julia was Hellman's beloved girlhood friend, an idealistic young woman who becomes a member of the Resistance in Germany. At the movie's dramatic center, Hellman (played by Jane Fonda) meets Julia (played by Vanessa Redgrave) at a café outside the Berlin train station. With some reluctance, Hellman has agreed to make this detour to Berlin in order to smuggle a large sum of cash, cash meant for the Resistance, to Julia. The two women, aware they are being watched, chat amicably as the exchange is made (the money is in Hellman's hat), catching up as old friends might. They talk about Hellman's plays and about Dashiell Hammett, her lover. Julia is on crutches; she has already lost a leg in the fight. She tells Hellman that she now has a baby, a little girl she named Lillian, who is being cared for by a baker's family just over the border, out of harm's way. The money is exchanged, and the women part. Not long after, Hellman learns that her beloved friend has been killed. She makes another trip to Europe—we see her going into bakeries in a number of small towns, inquiring and receiving only shrugs and sadly shaken heads. Hellman returns to New York and Dashiell Hammett (played in all his gruff glory by Jason Robards). The war begins, and the search for Julia's daughter cannot continue. In voice-over, Jane Fonda, as Lillian Hellman, sums up the meaning of the word *pentimento*: "Old paint on canvas sometimes becomes transparent," etc., etc. The film ends.

Beaming, my friend faced her group of seniors ready to receive their own charming reminiscences. "Isn't that true?" she said by way of beginning the discussion. "How sometimes as we age, we see the past in a new way?"

As my friend tells it, she was met with utter silence. A few of the ladies were smiling encouragingly, but many more were watching her rather sullenly. For a long moment, no one spoke. Then one woman, somewhat hunched and twisted in her chair, cried out, "What about the baby?"

"Julia's baby," another added indignantly.

My friend nodded, ready to begin the discussion. "Hellman never finds Julia's baby, does she?"

"Why not?" another lady called out.

Patiently, my friend explained that Hellman, of course, had looked for the baby—"We saw that, didn't we?"—but then the war came, and she couldn't go back to Europe. She never did find the child.

Again the silence and the sullen looks.

"That's terrible," someone said finally.

"That's ridiculous," said another.

It was too bad, my friend agreed. But that's what really happened. This was a memoir, she pointed out. It describes what really happened. (Although, of course, there's been much debate about the veracity of Hellman's own account of things.)

But the ladies were not appeased. "You can't do that," they argued. "You can't just forget about the baby. That makes a terrible story."

"The baby has to be somewhere."

There was nothing to be done. Each time my friend tried to move the conversation on—to the nature of memory, to the war, to how lovely Jane Fonda looked in that hat—the twisted old woman in the chair cried out, "What about the baby?" and the ladies' collective outrage rose again. At one point, a copy of *Pentimento* went flying through the air.

As my friend put it later, what the women in the senior center were saying was that they'd been given a story with a baby in it, and they damn well wanted that baby accounted for. And until that baby was accounted for, you could take your lovely metaphors and your dramatic suspense and your complex profundities about love and war and memory and go straight to hell with them. There was a baby missing, for Christ's sake.

Considering my own reaction to these accumulating rape scenes, I began to wonder if, after all this time, all this reading, after two degrees in literature and over thirty years teaching in departments of English and creative writing, I was, alas, no more sophisticated in my response to the written word than those outraged old ladies had been to the film. I began to wonder if I hated stumbling upon these rape scenes not because they were (artistically?) gratuitous or (morally?) misogynistic, but because I believed in the lives of those discarded women and girls more fully than their authors did.

I believed in them—the feisty little girl who pulled down some boy's pants, the skinny, sweet-faced child who is strangled—and because I believed in them, their suffering, their fear, their terrible deaths, pained me. I found myself mourning for them, for their families, long after their creators—the authors who had brought these women and girls to life, only to, quite graphically, destroy them—had moved on to make a larger point.

Doubtless these intelligent and serious authors *had* larger points, more important points, more profound points to make with their cruel and awful details, but for me, there was nothing more essential than the human suffering these graphic scenes described. Nothing more compelling than the unique life, and death, of these women and girls. *"What about the baby?"*

I was a disgrace to the academy, I thought, really sleepless now. An emotional, sentimental, simplistic reader. They should never let me teach.

A thought that immediately led me to recall another trend I'd begun to notice at the time, not in my casual reading but in the classroom: more and more over the course of those years, I found myself reading fiction by bright young women written in the voices of bright young men.

When I asked a group of undergraduate women writers about this, their response was immediate: "Everyone's afraid to write chick lit," they said. When I asked my female grad students the same question, they gave exactly the same reply: no one wants to write chick lit. Writing in a man's voice, these young writers seemed to believe, was the surest way to avoid that terrible label. A woman narrating the story of her life with an annoying boyfriend was chick lit. A man narrating the story of his life with an annoying woman was, well, *literature.*

A few weeks before this dark night of this reader's soul, I'd visited a large book club—a club, rarely enough, made up of both men and women readers—where fear of chick lit had also entered the discussion. If there was one thing the group strived strenuously to avoid, they told me, it was subjecting the men among them to "women's books." This group was after serious literature, they said, and they assured me that in this pursuit they made no distinction at all between male or female authors—citing Geraldine Brooks's *March* and Marilynne Robinson's *Gilead* and my own *Charming Billy,* three books they had recently discussed, as proof of their freedom from bias. Three books written by women, I had to point out, but about men.

Now I was beginning to suspect I'd never sleep.

The convergence of these two, perhaps imaginary, trends—raped and murdered girls in literary fiction, and young women writing literary fiction in the voices of men—began to stir in my heart far more worry than I'd bargained for.

Look, it's not surprising that young writers in MFA programs harbor a fascination for the work of their near peers—that is, new writers somewhat close to their own age who are "making it," publishing acclaimed first books or stories. While these students may indeed also look to the greats, to Shakespeare and Homer, Chekhov, Austen, James, Woolf, Faulkner, et al., they cannot be blamed for studying rather closely, as well, the new literary stars of the moment to see what they're up to, what it is about them that editors and reviewers love, perhaps, even to crib a bit of their style, their concerns, possibly their subject matter. When I was a grad student, Ann Beattie and Raymond Carver were the first on the list of writers we kept an eye on, and our workshops were filled with bad imitations—tight-lipped minimalism, ironic ennui, trailer parks, Kmarts, and empty swimming pools—as an unfortunate result.

But what happens when young women writers, checking out who's new, who's making it, stumble upon dead girls wrapped in plastic, hanging from trees, overpowered, mutilated, strangled?

The connection—the metaphor—became obvious, as metaphors will at 3:00 a.m. Young women writers will grow fearful—"We're all afraid of writing chick lit." They will be strangled. They will lose their voice.

Or maybe the savviest among them, in the spirit of "If you can't beat 'em, join 'em," will offer the world the rapee's point of view. Although a case can surely be made, I thought, that whether told by the abuser or the abused, the insidious appeal of it all—of these characterizations of women as victims, as somehow more interesting, more valued, more essential to plot when they are unconscious or traumatized, gone missing or found disemboweled—remains the same.

But wait, I thought (probably rolling over in bed): Surely, there's no conspiracy here. I am indeed a bad, sentimental reader, and were I a better one, I might see that these various rape scenes could also be an honest attempt by their authors to reflect reality, to explore the nature of evil, to illustrate the depravity that lurks just beyond the bedroom window or the placid golf course. Reviewers have pointed out that the three-hundred-page section of

Bolaño's novel that recounts in clinical detail the murder of hundreds of women and girls was inspired by the real-life epidemic of female homicides in Juárez. Can't these various references to the rape and murder of women be an attempt to acknowledge the travesty, to decry the sorry state of our violent selves? Doesn't a good writer have to show rape in all its precise and clinical detail in order to illuminate its horror?

Yes, but . . . I recalled Harriet Wasserman, my first literary agent and one of the wisest women I've ever known, wryly telling me about a visit she made to Germany. Every time she came upon a plaque or monument that referenced the Holocaust, she found herself, she said—only half joking—looking warily over her shoulder. Of course, these memorials were a way for the German people to acknowledge a terrible past, but for her, she said, these reminders conveyed only one message: we did this before, and we can do it again.

Never forget, after all, is a rallying cry when it's offered by the victims.

In the mouths of the perpetrators, it's a threat.

A dark night, as I say.

And in the morning, at my own desk, the question lingered: What's a woman writer to do? Be afraid, be very afraid? Join the apparent trend: rape sells? Try to make the point that she can write as well as any man about violence and abuse? Or—how about this?—let your distaste for these scenes, your motherly indignation, your outrage on behalf of your female students who have grown fearful of using a woman's voice, guide your hand, shape your story, infuse your characters. Strike back. Set the record straight. Remember the old feminist rallying cry, and use your own fiction to hold back the night.

The answer—and my entire, simple point here—is: No. Not at all. You must do nothing of the sort.

Here's Virginia Woolf on Charlotte Brontë:

> . . . it is clear [in *Jane Eyre*] that anger was tampering with the
> integrity of Charlotte Brontë the novelist. She left her story, to
> which her entire devotion was due, to attend to some personal
> grievance . . . Her imagination swerved from indignation and
> we feel it swerve . . . We feel the influence of fear in it . . .

There are many things that must be locked out of the room
(of one's own) where we write: friends and family, critics, bills,
trends in contemporary literature, to-do lists, even what we have
written in the past and what we might write in the future. But
chief among them is *a point to be made*—even when that point
has kept us up all night, fired our emotions, made us both angry
and sad, indignant and afraid.

"Remember," Flannery O'Connor said,

> that you don't write a story because you have an *idea* but be-
> cause you have a believable character . . . When you have a
> character he will create his own situation and his situation will
> suggest some kind of resolution as you get into it. Wouldn't it
> be better for you to discover a meaning in what you write than
> to impose one? Nothing you write will lack meaning because
> the meaning is in you.

"Writing fiction," Eudora Welty wrote,

> places the novelist and the crusader on opposite sides . . . We
> cannot in fiction set people to acting mechanically or carry-
> ing placards to make their sentiments plain. People are not
> Right and Wrong, Good and Bad, Black and White person-
> ified; flesh and blood and the sense of comedy object . . . the

novelist works neither to correct nor to condone, not at all to comfort, but to make what's told alive . . . Passion is the chief ingredient of good fiction. It flames right out of sympathy for the human condition and goes into all great writing . . . But to distort a work of passion for the sake of a cause is to cheat, and the end, far from justifying the means, is fairly sure to be lost with it.

And there's this from Henry James:

A novel is in its broadest definition a personal, a direct impression of life: that, to begin with, constitutes its value, which will be greater or less according to the intensity of the impression. But there will be no intensity at all, and therefore no value, unless there is freedom to feel and say. The tracing of a line to be followed, of a tone to be taken, of a form to be filled out, is a limitation of that freedom and a suppression of the very thing that we are most curious about.

I don't pretend that this is easy. Clearing your workroom of preformed ideas, especially ideas born of anger or fear—or indignation—requires a vigilance it is sometimes exhausting to sustain.

I recall another morning, when I was in the middle of writing the novel that was to become my sixth, *After This*. I had dropped my youngest off at his elementary school and was crossing the parking lot, when I ran into another mother, a woman I had known through the school for many years. We paused to catch up, as women do—as Julia and Lillian Hellman did, but without the Nazis—and my friend asked if I was writing another novel. (It's a question that always takes me by surprise—akin to, Are you still feeding your children?) I said yes, of course. And she laughed and said, "Is someone going to die in this one, too? All of your novels are about someone dying."

She was right—it's perfectly true. And, no doubt embarrassed by the truth of it, I said, "No, I'm writing a mystery."

She seemed impressed. "No kidding," she said.

"A murder mystery," I added, thinking we would both get the joke that murder mysteries, by definition, must be about someone dying.

She didn't. In fact, she said something like, "Oh, good."

And we went on our ways.

If only the laity knew what tsunamis of doubt these casual criticisms can set off in the still waters of our very shallow confidence.

Driving home to begin my writing day, I resolved never again to write about death. Never. From now on, no one dies. I resolved, in fact, to restore life to one of the characters in my half-completed novel, who, until that moment, had seemed fated to die in Vietnam. I never liked the idea of writing about a character who dies in Vietnam anyway, I thought—it was a cliché, an easy bit of melodrama. Too heavy by far. Far too short on irony. Uncool. Walking into the house, I was determined to bring the poor kid home alive, maybe even make the ending funny and shock the hell out of all those sarcastic readers who expect my books to be all Irish and mournful all the time. Ha, I thought. I'll show 'em.

My desk on that day, by the time I got to it, was not only covered with bills, student manuscripts, all of my previous books, all of everyone else's previous books, every review that has ever been written, every coed book club member I have ever met, every single one of my relatives, Tim O'Brien, Stephen Crane, and the selection committees for every major literary prize, but also an entire sorority of mothers from the carpool line rolling their eyes and asking, "Death again?"

I was, as you can imagine, a long while clearing them all out. But once I had done so, I saw that what I had before me was a novel that opened with a family seeking shelter from a Long Island hurricane, gathering in their basement. The father tells the children a war story; a weeping willow tree falls. Later, the mother and the daughter will visit the World's Fair to see the *Pietà*. They were a family bound for sorrow. The story demanded it. The characters demanded it. And with the room stripped at last of every other consideration, I had only the story and the characters to serve.

. . . if one reads those pages over [this is Woolf again] and marks that indignation, one sees that she [Brontë] will never get her genius expressed whole and entire. Her books will be deformed and twisted. She will write in a rage where she should write calmly. She will write foolishly where she should write wisely. She will write of herself where she should write of her characters.

She will write of herself where she should write of her characters. Another way of saying, perhaps, to hell with your ideas and philosophies and points to make, what about the human beings you have brought to life with your words? What about your characters, their joys and sorrows, triumphs, failings, hopes? What about the baby?

I was sorry to have stumbled across so many graphic references to rape in my reading life. They offended me. They discouraged me. They left me disappointed and afraid. And angry, really angry. But I never wrote about the phenomenon, or my distaste, or my worries, not in my fiction anyway, which is the only writing I do that matters.

I saved it for an essay.

MARY McCARTHY

I thought I had a vivid memory of when I was first introduced to Mary McCarthy. It was the early sixties, and she appeared as a guest on *The Jack Paar Program*. I was about ten.

The Jack Paar Program was a great favorite of my parents. They were both city-bred but had been exiled in adulthood to the dull suburbs of middle-class Long Island, and they seemed to think that Paar's urbane wit and eloquent guests provided us, their children, with a much-needed glimpse of New York intellectual life, city sophistication.

I thought I vividly recalled McCarthy's appearance on the show. I had two maiden aunts, career women in Manhattan, who, although they were hardly Vassar girls, were, I thought, very much like her. Confident, elegant, smart. I thought I remembered thinking—accurately, it turned out—that someday I would read the book she had written, but probably not for a very long while. It was, she said, about sex—how funny sex is.

I remember her saying this, and so I'm certain that as she said it, my parents, sitting behind me in our tiny living room, tsk-tsked at the notion—it was their usual and oft-repeated way of telling me that they disapproved of what someone on television had said, but not so vehemently that they wanted to get up and turn off the set.

I don't recall being surprised that Mary McCarthy, a woman, was a famous writer, or that the book she had written was a huge success.

So I was somewhat dismayed to discover only recently a YouTube clip of that long-ago interview. Dismayed because what I had not remembered was that, in introducing her, Paar had said, "It's been my impression in the past that women writers, however dainty their prose, on personal meeting are about as feminine as Ernest Borgnine in a steam bath. Mary McCarthy, however, on contact, is soft-spoken, twinkling, honest, and completely feminine."

I had not remembered this introduction. I had not remembered that Mary McCarthy, in that 1963 interview, with her purse held in the crook of her arm, was indeed soft-spoken, twinkling (twinkling!), honest, and completely feminine.

I had not remembered that my ten-year-old self was once offered these dueling portraits of the woman writer—the soft-spoken lady or the hairy ape—although I guess in the long run it didn't do me any harm. I wrote a novel at twelve anyway.

McCarthy said that "Every age has a keyhole to which its eye is pasted." Our current age can sometimes seem to be glued to a keyhole that shows it only itself. As we gaze, we fail to remember, or to acknowledge, the assumptions, the biases, the cultural, historical, emotional context in which past generations—not even long past—once lived and spoke and wrote.

Mary McCarthy lived and spoke and wrote, and held her own, at a time when all the forces of our culture had their big, wing-tipped feet in the aisle, ready to trip her up. She was a woman who wrote—about women and men and sex and politics, about Florence and Venice and Vietnam—not in an age wary enough of its prejudices to muffle the sneer beneath the term *woman writer*, but at a time when the sneer was the sustenance of the boys' club that was not just the literary life but the culture at large.

It's good to remember this. To remember what she was a product of, and what she was up against. To celebrate, paraphrasing Auden's words about Yeats, that if she was, at times, silly—soft-spoken, twinkling, feminine—her gift survived it all.

ONLY CONNECT (EVENTUALLY)

This is the simplest—and perhaps most simplistic—advice I can offer a fledgling novelist: while in the midst of composing your novel, for God's sake, read what you've already written.

Read it often—daily, if need be. Read it all. Read it thoroughly. Read it always with a keen and critical eye.

I suspect this advice applies to the creation of short stories and poems and plays, as well, but it's my experience that novelists are the most reluctant to follow it. We like to say, "Well, I've finished the first six chapters of my novel." Or, "I only have three more chapters to write." We like to feel the heft of our "first two hundred pages," warm from the printer—like fresh-baked bread—and say, "Here's what I've completed so far." Meaning by "completed," of course, finished, perfected. Don't have to read it again. Don't have to change a thing.

The truth of the matter is this: until the work of your heart and your mind and your hands meets the bookbinders' work of paper and ink and paste or thread, your novel is a fluid thing, an unpredictable thing, and every page, every paragraph, every sentence you add runs the delightful risk of changing everything that has come before. Read what you've already written before you add something new. And then read it again in the light of what's been added. Add more. Subtract some. Repeat. It's the simplest advice I can offer. Here's my thinking:

As will soon become clear, I am no Shakespeare scholar. But as a college sophomore I took a Shakespeare course from a mild-mannered professor who looked more like an insurance sales-man than an academic: crew cut, horn-rimmed glasses, plaid sport coat. On the first day of class, he introduced the syllabus by saying, "In this class we will be rereading the Henry plays," which caused some consternation in the ranks. This was a lower-level, introductory Shakespeare course at a state college, after all.

When someone in the class pointed this out, adding that many of us had not yet read the history plays even *once*, the pro-fessor listened patiently, nodded, and said, "Exactly."

And then he said again, "In this course we will be rereading the Henry plays."

A year later, I took another class in the history plays at a uni-versity in England. There, the professor actually looked the part: long nose, wild white hair, black scholastic robe, and sneering Oxford accent. He began by asking us how many times we had read the plays: once? twice? three times? He didn't seem to want a show of hands; the British students around me just nodded when their number was called. Then he looked down at his lec-ture notes—I don't think he ever looked up from them again—and said, dismissively, "Your education hasn't even begun."

In the years since then, I have indeed reread the Henry plays, read about them, even brought bits and pieces of them into the classroom now and then. I've seen the various film versions. And I've seen the plays performed—in New York, in London, in San Diego, in Washington, D.C.

I recall a particularly affecting performance at the Shake-speare Theater Company in D.C., in 2004, just about the time the United States was coming to terms with the fantasy of Iraq's hidden weapons of mass destruction. At the end of the play, King Henry speaks these lines:

> Three knights upon our party slain today,
> A noble earl, and many a creature else
> Had been alive at this hour
> If, like a Christian, thou hadst truly borne
> Betwixt our armies true intelligence.

In Washington, D.C., in 2004, these lines made the audience gasp—you could hear it, even see the actors pause as they heard it—the phrase reverberating from that field in Shrewsbury to this inside-the-Beltway theater: *If, like a Christian, thou hadst truly borne / Betwixt our armies true intelligence.*

I'm not a Shakespeare scholar, but I love the Henry plays for their wit, their marvelous characters (Hal and Hotspur and Falstaff), for their language (of course), their shapeliness, and their rich humanity—all the things that Shakespeare did pretty well. If, as I once heard the playwright Romulus Linney argue, all drama is family drama, then the Henry plays are among the greatest and most thorough, most complex and most authentic, of family dramas: fathers and sons and siblings, husbands and wives and daughters.

So when I was devising a reading course for my MFA students in the coming-of-age novel, I knew I wanted to begin with *Henry IV*. Preparing for the class, I reread the play, reread the penciled side notes I had made in my college Shakespeare text, reread some criticism. A week before we were to discuss *Part 1* in class (we were also going to discuss the fiction my MFA students had written modeled after the play—which, it turned out, was marvelous), I came home from an early-morning appointment at the eye doctor and realized I could do no work until my dilated pupils returned to normal. I hate having the television on in the daytime; nevertheless, I made a cup of tea and, in order not to feel like too much of a goof-off, found the BBC's 2010 take on the history plays, *The Hollow Crown*. I watched *Part 1* and was well into *Part 2* when I slowly began to see a connection, a symmetry, in the plays that I had never noticed before.

As you'll recall, Prince Hal and his father, Henry IV, have a rather difficult relationship. Hal's a slacker, hanging around in pubs with whores and clowns and good old Sir John Falstaff. Hal claims he pretends to be a lowlife so that his star will shine all the brighter when he gives up that life and ascends to the throne. His father's pretty sure he's just a lowlife. Hal does briefly redeem himself on that field at Shrewsbury in *Part 1*, but Dad still isn't convinced his eldest son, and heir, is any good at all. In act 4, scene 5 of *Henry IV, Part 2*, Prince Hal arrives at his ailing father's bedside and mistakes him for dead. The crown lies upon the pillow beside his father's head. Prince Hal takes it. He says:

> My gracious Lord, my father,
> This sleep is sound indeed. This is a sleep
> That from this golden rigol hath divorced
> So many English kings. Thy due from me
> Is tears and heavy sorrows of the blood,
> Which nature, love and filial tenderness
> Shall, oh dear father, pay thee plenteously.
> My due from thee is this imperial crown,
> Which, as immediate from thy place and blood,
> Derives itself to me.

Hal puts on the crown and exits. His father then wakes up and sees that his crown is missing. He calls to his men, who explain that the prince was just there. They call for Hal, who returns to his father's chamber, the crown still on his head.

"I never thought to hear you speak again," he tells his father—somewhat nonplussed, you might say. The king replies:

> Thy wish was father, Harry, to that thought.
> I stay too long by thee; I weary thee,
> Dost thou so hunger for mine empty chair
> That thou wilt needs invest thee with my honors
> Before thy hour be ripe? Oh, foolish youth,
> Thou seekest the greatness that will overwhelm thee . . .
> Thou hast stol'n that which after some few hours
> Were thine without offense, and at my death
> Thou hast sealed up my expectation.
> Thy life did manifest thou loved'st me not,
> And thou wilt have me die assured of it.

This is, of course, a pivotal moment in the play: the dying father putting a seal on his bad opinion of his profligate or, perhaps, completely innocent son. (There are all kinds of opinions about this—Harold Bloom thinking Hal is a villain, a hypocrite, others believing, some thoroughly, some partially, in his virtue. The fact that you can believe both things about Hal, that you can both hope he is noble but never really trust that he is, is, for me, part of the brilliance of the play—and, of course, the fun of all presidential elections.)

After enduring a bit more of his father's contempt ("Harry the Fifth is crowned. Up! vanity, Down, royal state . . . !"), Harry attempts to explain. He tells his father:

> Coming to look on you, thinking you dead,
> And dead almost, my liege, to think you were,

I spake unto this crown as having sense,
And thus upbraided it: "The care on thee depending
Hath fed upon the body of my father;
Therefore thou best of gold art worst of gold:
Other, less fine in carat, is more precious,
Preserving life in med'cine potable;
But thou, most fine, most honored, most renowned
Hast eat thy bearer up." Thus, my most royal liege,
Accusing it, I put it on my head
To try with it, as with an enemy
That had before my face murdered my father . . .

"Do we believe this?" I recall my Oswego professor—or was it my British professor?—asking the class. Is Hal speaking truly—I put on the crown only to try with it, as with an enemy —or is he offering a slick cover-up for the vanity and ambition that made him don the crown the minute he thought his father was dead? Of course, there are endless ways to look at it—that's Shakespeare—but what I saw on that cold afternoon, when I watched the play again with dilated eyes, was that Hal's explanation was, actually, pure Falstaff—that it echoed and paralleled, was inextricably connected to, the time the young prince has spent with the fat man. How had I not seen this before?

As you may recall, early in *Part 1*, Hal and his friend Poins play a trick on old Falstaff. They agree to go with him to Gad's Hill to rob some pilgrims, but they fail to appear. Then, after the robbery, in disguise they set on Falstaff. Falstaff flees in terror, but when he comes back to the pub, he tells an elaborate tale of how he fended off his five, six, eight attackers. When Hal reveals that he and Poins had been the attackers and had seen Falstaff flee for his life, the large knight makes a quick adjustment in his tale, spinning it:

By the Lord, I knew you as well as he that made you. Why, hear you, my masters, was it for me to kill the heir apparent? Should I turn upon the true prince? Why, thou knowest I am as valiant as Hercules, but beware instinct. The lion will not touch the true prince. Instinct is a great matter. I was now a coward on instinct.

And again, in *Part 2*, Hal overhears Falstaff disparaging him to Doll Tearsheet, a prostitute. Hal confronts Falstaff with his disloyalty:

PRINCE: You whoreson candle-mine, you, how vilely did you speak of me . . .

FALSTAFF: Didst thou hear me?

PRINCE: Yea, and you knew me as you did when you ran away by Gad's Hill. You knew I was at your back, and spoke it on purpose to try my patience.

FALSTAFF: No, no, not so. I did not think thou wast within hearing.

PRINCE: I shall drive you, then, to confess the willful abuse, and then I know how to handle you.

FALSTAFF: No abuse, Hal, o' mine honor, no abuse.

PRINCE: Not to dispraise me and call me pantler and bread-chipper and I know not what?

FALSTAFF: No abuse, Hal.

POINS: No abuse?

FALSTAFF: No abuse, Ned, i' th' world, honest Ned, none. I dispraised him before the wicked [meaning Doll Tearsheet] that the wicked [to the Prince] might not fall in love with thee, in which doing I have done the part of a careful friend and a true subject, and thy father is to give me thanks for it. No abuse, Hal. None . . .

I suppose I'd always thought that Falstaff's glib backtracking in each of these scenes was mere comic relief, just another delightful illustration of Falstaff's slippery character. But watching the play yet again, and with new eyes, so to speak, I saw how Hal's heart-felt speech to his dying father—his excuse, his explanation for tak-ing the crown—is the same verbal quick-change artistry Falstaff employs earlier in the play, how it is, perhaps, the best lesson the young prince has learned from the master reprobate. Falstaff, the spinmeister, uses this verbal sleight of hand, comically, to save face. Hal uses it—insidiously, cravenly, desperately—to regain his father's love in the last moments of the old man's life.

It may have taken me fifteen or so readings of the plays, half a dozen viewings, and forty years to make this connection, but, having made it, I was filled with awe once again at how beau-tifully Shakespeare orchestrates his plays, provides us, across two full-length dramas, with nothing inconsequential: no mere comic relief, no mere treading of narrative water, no mere char-acter development. How everything in Shakespeare resonates, returns, connects.

My point is this: If we are the very first readers of our own novels—and how can it be otherwise?—then why wouldn't we want to be the most careful, the most dogged, the most patient, as well as the most eager of readers? Why wouldn't we want to go over again and again what we've already set down, just as a scholar would, looking for consequence, looking for pattern, sowing the psychological seeds in one scene that will blossom in another, as well as culling those seeds that fail to bloom. Adding as we go, yes, of course, but also clarifying, revising, what we wrote last month in light of what we wrote yesterday, connecting what we wrote yesterday with what we added today.

And there's that word again: *connect*. And here comes E. M. Forster.

I confess that I've bludgeoned a fair number of novels-in-progress (and their authors) with his now all-too-familiar injunction. To be fair, Forster proposed it, I think, not as writing advice, but as life advice. And to be fairer still—we should all be fair to our fellow novelists—here's the context in which the phrase appears.

In *Howards End*, free-spirited Margaret Schlegel has agreed to marry the sedate widower Henry Wilcox. Forster says of their alliance:

> . . . there was nothing excessive about her love-affair. Good-humor was the dominant note of her relations with Mr. Wilcox, or, as I must now call him, Henry. Henry did not encourage romance, and she was not a girl to fidget for it. An acquaintance had become a lover, might become a husband, but would retain all that she had noted in the acquaintance; and love must confirm an old relation rather than reveal a new one. In this spirit she promised to marry him.

Forster then describes their "first real love scene"—a turn on the parade—that ends with this:

> They walked ahead briskly. The parade and the road after it were well lighted, but it was darker in Aunt Julie's garden. As they were going up by the side-paths, through some rhododendrons, Mr. Wilcox, who was in front, said "Margaret" rather huskily, turned, dropped his cigar, and took her in his arms.
>
> She was startled, and nearly screamed, but recovered herself at once, and kissed with genuine love the lips that were pressed against her own. It was their first kiss, and when it was over he saw her safely to the door and rang the bell for her, but disappeared into the night before the maid answered it. On looking back, the incident displeased her. It was so isolated.

Nothing in their previous conversation had heralded it, and worse still, no tenderness ensued. If a man cannot lead up to passion, he can at all events lead down from it, and she had hoped, after her complaisance, for some interchange of tender words. But he had hurried away as if ashamed.

One chapter later, this brief reflection, this awkward, isolated, unconnected first kiss, engenders the philosophical storm that produces the famous two words:

Margaret greeted her lord with peculiar tenderness on the morrow. Mature as he was, she might yet be able to help him to the building of the rainbow bridge that should connect the prose in us with the passion. Without it we are meaningless fragments, half monks, half beasts, unconnected arches that have never joined into a man. With it love is born, and alights on the highest curve, glowing against the grey, sober against the fire. Happy the man who sees from either aspect the glory of these outspread wings. The roads of his soul lie clear, and he and his friends shall find easy going.

It was hard going in the road of Mr. Wilcox's soul. From boyhood he had neglected it. "I am not a fellow who bothers about my own inside." Outwardly he was cheerful, reliable, and brave; but within, all had reverted to chaos, ruled, so far as it was ruled at all, by an incomplete asceticism. Whether as a boy, husband, or widower, he had always the sneaking belief that bodily passion is bad, a belief that is desirable only when held passionately. Religion had confirmed him. The words that were read aloud on Sunday to him and to other respectable men were the words that once kindled the souls of St. Catherine and St. Francis into white-hot hatred of the carnal. He could not be as the saints and love the Infinite with seraphic ardour, but he could be a little ashamed of loving a wife. And it was here that Margaret hoped to help him.

It did not seem so difficult. She need trouble him with no gift of her own. She would only point out the salvation that was latent in his own soul, and in the soul of every man. Only connect! That was the whole of her sermon. Only connect the prose and the passion, and both will be exalted, and human love will be seen at its height. Live in fragments no longer. Only connect, and the beast and the monk, robbed of the isolation that is life to either, will die.

Only connect. Life advice, in the novel, and perhaps in Forster's own life as a gay man in Edwardian England, but it can be nicely taken out of context to serve as craft advice, as well. I don't think Forster would object. After all, he took the two words out of context himself when he used them as the epigraph for *Howards End*, and again when he had them engraved on his tombstone, a place that doesn't leave much room for context.

It is advice that Forster himself followed brilliantly in his own work—evident in the logical connections Miss Schlegel makes about her intended: his boyhood, his incomplete asceticism, his being, consequently, a little ashamed of loving a wife.

Or consider the opening sentence of *A Passage to India*:

Except for the Marabar Caves—and they are twenty miles off—the city of Chandrapore presents nothing extraordinary.

Those of you who know the novel will immediately recognize how, in this first sentence, plot and theme are struck and will reverberate, through event and discourse, to the novel's end.

"Except for the Marabar Caves . . ."

We hear nothing more of these caves until nearly seventy pages later. Young Dr. Aziz, a Muslim intern, has tea with two charming Englishwomen, the lovely Miss Quested and the elderly Mrs. Moore, and he impulsively invites the ladies to his house—which he thinks of as "a detestable shanty near a low bazaar." When they accept, he panics:

> He thought again of his bungalow with horror. Good heavens, the stupid girl had taken him at his word! What was he to do? "Yes, all that is settled," he cried. "I invited you all to see me in the Marabar Caves."

Another sixty pages later, we read:

> The caves are readily described. A tunnel eight feet long, five feet high, three feet wide, leads to a circular chamber about twenty feet in diameter. This arrangement occurs again and again throughout the group of hills, this is all, this is a Marabar cave. Having seen one such cave, having seen two, having seen three, four, fourteen, twenty-four, the visitor returns to Chandrapore uncertain whether he has had an interesting experience or a dull one or any experience at all. He finds it difficult to discuss the caves, or to keep them apart in his mind, for the pattern never varies, and no carving, not even a bees'-nest or a bat distinguishes one from another. Nothing, nothing attaches to them, and their reputation—for they have one—does not depend on human speech.

Aziz reluctantly arranges an excursion to the caves for a picnic. He has, in his anxiousness, hired a large retinue of servants, who rush into the first cave along with Aziz and the ladies, causing a crisis for old Mrs. Moore.

A Marabar cave had been horrid as far as Mrs. Moore was concerned, for she had nearly fainted in it . . . There are some exquisite echoes in India; there is the whisper round the dome of Bijapur; there are the long, solid sentences that voyage through the air at Mandu, and return unbroken to their creator. The echo in a Marabar cave is not like these, it is entirely devoid of distinction. Whatever is said, the same monotonous noise replies, and quivers up and down the walls until it is absorbed into the roof. "Boum," is the sound as far as the human alphabet can express it, or "bou-oum, or "ou-boum"—utterly dull. Hope, politeness, the blowing of a nose, the squeak of a boot, all produce, "boum."

No, she [Mrs. Moore] did not wish to repeat that experience. The more she thought over it, the more disagreeable and frightening it became . . . The crush and the smells she could forget, but the echo began in some indescribable way to undermine her hold on life. Coming at a moment when she chanced to be fatigued, it had managed to murmur, "Pathos, piety, courage— they exist, but are identical, and so is filth. Everything exists, nothing has value." If one had spoken vileness in that place, or quoted lofty poetry, the comment would have been the same— "ou-boum."

One hundred and sixty-five pages after we encounter the novel's opening line, "Except for the Marabar Caves," these caves undermine an old woman's hold on life. One hundred and eighty pages later, a brief exchange in one of them leads to a chain of events that undermines the empire itself.

Except for the Marabar Caves.

Since, as far as I know, E. M. Forster was never sent out on a book tour and never, then, asked the ubiquitous book-tour question: "Do you plan out your novels before you write them, or do you just make them up as you go along?" it is impossible for us to know if those first words of the novel were, indeed, the first words he wrote or if he began the novel elsewhere and then went back, once he saw the role the caves would play in his plot, and added them.

It's possible to imagine, for instance, that he actually began the novel with Aziz and the opening lines of chapter 2: "Abandoning his bicycle, which fell before a servant could catch it, the young man sprang up on to the veranda. He was all animation."

Lines a writing workshop would no doubt deem a much livelier opening, much more cinematic. And more efficient, too, starting with your main character rather than an unpromising description of a town—a fictional town, at that—that offers, except for the caves, nothing extraordinary.

While composing *A Passage to India*, Forster wrote to a friend, "When I began the book, I thought of it as a little bridge of sympathy between East and West, but this conception has had to go, my sense of truth forbids anything so comfortable."

Evidence, perhaps, that even if Forster had certain ideas about the novel in the beginning, he allowed those ideas to change as he wrote—and that the first line was forged not in a "planning out" session before the writing began, but in the fire of the composition of the novel itself.

But even if that first sentence were indeed the very first sentence he put down in composing his novel, surely he could not have known, at the beginning, the resonance those words would have—*nothing extraordinary*—once his characters reached those caves: *nothing, nothing adheres to them . . . everything exists, nothing has value.*

Did the first line shape those later sentences, or did the appearance of those later sentences inspire Forster to go back and reshape that first line?

Does it matter?

Honestly, why do readers care so much about whether the author knew the whole novel from the start or went back and changed it as he went along? The effect, the effect of connectedness, is there in the finished work. Isn't that the artistry? Isn't that the thrill? Do we have to go into the studio and examine the paint-smudged rags before we can appreciate the masterpiece in a museum?

Consider some famous opening sentences that just might have been tweaked, changed, or added entirely after the composing of the novel had begun—even, perhaps, after much of the novel was finished:

- This is the saddest story I have ever heard.
- He was an old man who fished alone in a skiff in the Gulf Stream, and he had gone eighty-four days now without taking a fish.
- When he was nearly thirteen, my brother Jem got his arm badly broken at the elbow.

"Story," Forster writes in *Aspects of the Novel*, "is a narrative of events arranged in their time sequence." Time features in every story, of course, and is essential to it, of course, but the author, to paraphrase Forster, hovers above the story, not in it. In the novel itself, the author's time is meaningless. Take five months to write your novel, or five years. The reader will enter the novel on the first page and finish it with the last, with no thought of the time you've spent on this sentence as opposed to that one. Write your first chapter in February and discover in June that it's really your second chapter and then recast it again in November as the third—for the reader who picks it up a year later, or forty years later, it is, and always will be, the third chapter of the novel.

My agent Harriet Wasserman used to assure me when I

feared I was taking too long between books that no book review ever began: "This novel would have been better if it came out two years ago." No one, she said, remembers when something was published; they only remember what was published.

What is memorable, then, is not the saga of how the author knew, or didn't know, the story when she began to compose it. What is memorable is the sense of inevitability, of nothing superfluous, nothing wasted, of meaning and consequence revealing itself, resonating, page after page after page, in the completed work.

Forster calls story "a narrative of events arranged in time sequence," but he goes on to say that plot "is also a narrative of events, the emphasis falling on causality. 'The king died and then the queen died' is a story. 'The king died and then the queen died of grief' is a plot."

This sense of causality reveals itself to the reader page by page, in time, but that's not necessarily how it reveals itself to the writer. The author may sense that the caves will feature prominently in his story and so mention them in the first line. He may also discover on page 76, or 133, or 250 that the caves are of great consequence in his story and so then go back and insert them into the first line.

As we compose our novels, we tend to look for this sense of causality, of consequence, in large arcs as we desperately work out our plots. But we need to reread what we've already written in order to look for it in all things, large and small—the development of character, for instance, the development of Prince Hal's character, for instance, at the feet of Sir John Falstaff.

Or observe Forster again, in *A Passage to India*.

Here is Aziz, all animation (as we're told in our first glimpse of him), meeting Mr. Fielding, the British director of the college, before the fateful tea party:

He [Fielding] was dressing after a bath when Dr. Aziz was announced. Lifting up his voice, he shouted from the bedroom, "Please make yourself at home." The remark was unpremeditated, like most of his actions; it was what he felt inclined to say.

(Character development.)

To Aziz it had a very definite meaning. "May I really, Mr. Fielding? It's very good of you," he called back; "I like unconventional behavior so extremely." His spirits flared up.

(Character development becomes *consequential*: Fielding's unpremeditated remark causes Aziz's spirits to flare up.)

He glanced around the living-room. Some luxury in it, but no order—nothing to intimidate poor Indians.

(Now setting becomes consequential: it is not intimidating; thus, animated Aziz speaks freely, warmly.)

"The fact is I have long wanted to meet you," Aziz continued. "I have heard so much about your warm heart from the Nawab Bahadu. But where is one to meet in a wretched hole like Chandrapore?" He came close up to the door. "When I was greener here, I'll tell you what. I used to wish you to fall ill so that we could meet that way." They laughed, and encouraged by his success he began to improvise.

(More consequence: success leads to improvisation.)

"I said to myself, How does Mr. Fielding look this morning? Perhaps pale. And the Civil Surgeon is pale too, he will not

be able to attend upon him when the shivering commences.
I should have been sent for instead. Then we would have had
jolly talks, for you are a celebrated student of Persian poetry."

"You know me by sight, then?"

"Of course, of course. You know me?"

"I know you very well by name."

"I have been here such a short time, and always in the bazaar. No wonder you have never seen me, and I wonder you
know my name. I say, Mr. Fielding?"

"Yes?"

"Guess what I look like before you come out. That will be
a kind of game."

"You're five feet nine inches high," said Fielding, surmising
this much through the ground glass of the bedroom door.

"Jolly good. What next? Have I not a venerable white
beard?"

"Blast!"

"Anything wrong?"

"I've stamped on my last collar stud."

"Take mine, take mine."

"Have you a spare one?"

"Yes, yes, one minute."

"Not if you're wearing it yourself."

"No, no, one in my pocket." Stepping aside, so that his
outline might vanish, he wrenched off his collar, and pulled
out of his shirt the back stud, a gold stud, which was part of
a set that his brother-in-law had brought him from Europe.
"Here it is," he cried.

"Come in with it if you don't mind the unconventionality."

"One minute again." Replacing his collar, he prayed
that it would not spring up at the back during tea. Fielding's

bearer, who was helping him to dress, opened the door for him.

Twenty pages later, the tea has ended, the trip to the caves proposed. Ronny, the insufferable City Magistrate, son of Mrs. Moore and fiancé of Miss Quested, asks the women on the ride home, "What was that about the caves?"

Miss Quested explains, ". . . your delightful doctor has decided on a picnic, instead of a party in his house; we are to meet him out there . . ."

"Out where?" asked Ronny.

"The Marabar Caves."

"Well, I'm blessed," he murmured after a pause. "Did he descend to any details?"

"He did not. If you had spoken to him, we could have arranged them."

He shook his head, laughing.

"Have I said anything funny?"

"I was only thinking how the worthy doctor's collar climbed up his neck."

"I thought you were discussing the caves."

"So I am. Aziz was exquisitely dressed, from tie-pin to spats, but he had forgotten his back collar-stud, and there you have the Indian all over: inattention to detail; the fundamental slackness that reveals the race."

Another, less careful novelist, busily building his plot—getting his characters to the caves—might easily have forgotten the missing back collar stud. After all, it has already served its purpose as part of an effective character sketch; it has already demonstrated Aziz's animation, his overeagerness to please, his generosity and his innocence . . . a nice gesture, a nice detail, a worthy moment in and of itself, we might tell E.M. in a workshop . . . but good old "only connect" Forster is not content with details that merely characterize, illustrate, tread narrative water; he wants *consequence*, as well.

Because Fielding makes an unpremeditated remark, Aziz's spirits soar; because animated Aziz's spirits are soaring, and the setting is so unintimidating, and he has so longed to meet Fielding, Aziz offers his own back collar stud (blindly, you could say) to his new, as yet unseen, friend. Because Aziz has given away his back collar stud, his collar keeps rising during the tea in which he proposes the trip to the caves, and a British official is confirmed in his opinion of the subjugated race . . . an opinion that resounds and reverberates after the incident that marks the turning point of the novel.

The inattentive reader, the reluctant reader—and isn't that, increasingly, becoming all of us?—might well have been content never to hear about that back collar stud again after its first appearance. The inattentive reader might well have forgotten about it as soon as the scene ended. No loss, really: the plot of the novel still marches on. But if that inattentive or reluctant reader is the very first reader of this novel—is, in other words, its author—then that delightful shimmer of connectedness, that momentary glimpse of the complexity, the pathos, the hope, and the misunderstanding that is at the heart of all human interactions, will be lost forever. It will not be in the book at all. And the novel will be lesser for it.

Forster says in *Aspects of the Novel* that the ideal reader brings two things to the novel: memory and intelligence.

Intelligence first. The intelligent novel-reader, unlike the inquisitive one who just runs his eye over a new fact, mentally picks it up. He sees it from two points of view: isolated, and related to the other facts that he has read on previous pages. Probably he does not understand it, but he does not expect to do so yet awhile.

If you think of yourself as your own first reader, then Forster's description might read this way, as well: The intelligent novel-writer, as opposed to the one who just hopes to be finished, mentally picks up each new fact he adds to his novel. He sees each new fact from two points of view: isolated, and related to the other facts he has written on previous pages. Probably he does not understand it, but he does not expect to do so yet for a while . . .

Memory and intelligence, Forster goes on to say, are closely related:

> for unless we remember, we cannot understand. If by the time the queen dies we have forgotten the king we will never make out what killed her. The plot-maker expects us to remember, we expect him to leave no loose ends. Every action or word ought to count; it ought to be economical and spare; even when complicated it should be organic and free of dead matter. And over it, as it unfolds, will hover the memory of the reader (that dull glow of the mind of which intelligence is the advancing edge), and the memory of the reader will constantly rearrange and reconsider, seeing new clues, new chains of cause and effect, and the final sense will not be of clues or chains, but of something aesthetically compact . . .

Try it this way: And over it, as it unfolds, will hover the memory of the writer, and the memory of the writer—enhanced by the writer's ability to reread his own work—will constantly rearrange and reconsider what has already been written, seeing new clues, new chains of cause and effect, until the final sense will not be of clues or chains, but of something aesthetically compact with what follows.

In other words, the intelligence and memory that the perfect reader applies to the masterwork is equal to the intelligence and memory that the writer applies to the work-in-progress.

Here's Eudora Welty in *One Writer's Beginnings*:

> Writing a story or a novel is one way of discovering *sequence* in experience, of stumbling upon cause and effect . . . Connections slowly emerge. Like distant landmarks you are approaching, cause and effect begin to align themselves, draw closer together. Experiences too indefinite of outline in themselves to be recognized for themselves connect and are identified as a larger shape. And suddenly a light is thrown back, as when your train makes a curve, showing that there has been a mountain of meaning rising behind you on the way you've come, is rising there still, proven now through retrospect.

For the novelist in the midst of composing a novel, rereading is retrospect; to revisit what has already been set down is to provide oneself with the opportunity to glimpse that mountain of meaning rising behind.

Subject as we are to time, we human beings can only return to prior events, to the beginning of things, to the pivotal moment or the trivial one, in memory. We can only look for connections and guess at them. We can reinterpret, even put a Falstaff-like spin on things, but we cannot change what has already occurred. The novelist at her desk, in the midst of composition, is free of such constraints. She can, indeed, relive the pivotal incident; she can, in fact, remake it, reshaping it to match its consequences; she can tweak the trivial moment until it resounds down the years;

she can turn a barely noticed character trait into an unavoidable, already-composed fate; she can not only return to discover what Frank O'Connor calls the moment after which nothing else is ever the same, but can return and insert that moment—if only she will reread what she has already set down.

Here's Shakespeare again, from *Hamlet* this time, act 4, scene 1:

> Sure, he that made us with such large discourse,
> Looking before and after, gave us not
> That capability and godlike reason
> To fust in us unused.

I am not making a pitch for artifice, manipulation, or trickery, but rather for discovery. The kind of discovery that the attentive, eager reader makes, sometimes inadvertently, sometimes arduously, when rereading a great work of literature.

Prince Hal's words (or excuses) at his father's deathbed did not become Falstaffian the moment I recognized them as such: they'd been Falstaffian all along. It only remained for me, the reader, to uncover through repeated encounters with the play the connections that were always there.

I think this is true of the way we often uncover the subtleties—and even the not-so-subtleties—of our own work, because the nature of our art is such that every draft, even the first one, stirs our unconscious understanding.

Think of it: language is the writer's sole tool. We really have nothing else. But it is a tool that contains our entire experience of the world: our background, our heritage, our unique biographies. Who taught you the language in which you write? Whose voice was the first one you heard? Where and when? What intonations, rhythms, clichés, repetitions did you take in with your mother's milk?

When we write, when we rely on that single tool called language to create a new world, we evoke those early voices—and all subsequent voices, as well, everything we have heard, everything we have read: music, poetry, prayer, memory, story, conversation, song, argument, exchange, proclamations of love and grief and outrage and opinion. We call on everything that has shaped not only the way we speak but the way we think, because language is, as well, the way we speak to ourselves, plan, sort out, anticipate, narrate, worry, and, of course, remember.

And that's just the personal, the biographical, the *practical* aspect of the words we choose. There's also etymology to consider, root words and idioms, and whatever meanings and associations, rhythms and sounds, have clung to the words we use as they were passed on to us from the Latin or the Greek, the Persian or the Anglo-Saxon, from the questioning grunts and assuring coos of our first, hairy ancestors.

To shape a single sentence, then, to shape a scene, a character, a bit of exposition, is to evoke all these things, and so it should not surprise us that any single sentence we write in our effort to conjure a new world with words carries the possibility of untold depths, unforeseen complexities, subtle meanings, potential consequences, unplanned delights. Every new sentence we write offers the possibility of adding to our story not only the new fact we had planned to add but something else, something more, something that we can't recognize as we set the words down—or can recognize only as a stab in the dark, a forging ahead, an intuition—but that later rereading can actually reveal. The thing we didn't know we knew—about our story, our character, about how one moment connects to another—until we began to reread.

Of course, every sentence we add also carries the possibility of introducing shallowness, simplemindedness, meaninglessness, dead matter, and blind alleys, and often this, too, can only be discovered by rereading. We go over what we have already written not only to excise these mistakes and misdirections, but also, at some point, to dismantle the scaffolding, so to speak, that allows us to scale our novel while it is still under construction: those paragraphs, for instance, that we set down before we know our characters, or our stories, fully, notes to ourselves but not necessarily to the reader, or those multipage scenes full of careening dialogue that seem, at first, to be inspired, but prove to be, on cool rereading, repetitive and unnecessary—no need for a description of the whole meal, from grocery-store excursion to the chopping and the mixing and the setting of the table, and would you like some more gravy and so glad you could come and thanks so much for inviting me, when the single, spoken exchange at the end of the evening, "I leave for Zanzibar in the morning," might more efficiently, and dramatically, be delivered in a text message before the meal begins. No doubt the entire meal had to be written in order to make this clear to the author, but for the reader—as rereading will prove—the single line will do.

Eliminate, as you reread, six words from every page—or ten or fifty; see what you can do without and what you can't.

But no amount of trimming and revising, deleting and tweaking, will make the rereading worthwhile if we don't, also, teach ourselves to notice as we read—to pay attention to the words we have already put down as if we were encountering them for the first time. There is a difference between doggedly rereading the same words and allowing ourselves, as we read, to hear and see them anew.

Here's Margaret Schlegel again, thinking of Henry:

> . . . there was one quality in Henry for which she was never
> prepared, however much she reminded herself of it: his obtuse-
> ness. He simply did not notice things . . . he never noticed

the lights and shades that exist in the greyest conversation, the finger-posts, the milestones, the collisions, the illimitable views. Once . . . she scolded him about it. He was puzzled, but replied with a laugh: "My motto is Concentrate. I've no intention of frittering away my strength on that sort of thing." "It isn't frittering away the strength," she protested. "It's enlarging the space in which you may be strong."

Rereading your own work-in-progress is not so much a matter of concentrating on what you've already said—it's learning to notice the lights and shades, the illimitable views that exist in the grayest conversations, the simplest incidents. It's enlarging the space in which your novel may be strong.

My Shakespeare professors, both the mild-mannered guy from upstate New York and the third-generation literary scholar from Oxford, had, I think, the same goal in mind for us when they insisted that Shakespeare must not be read but reread. The goal was to allow us to uncover, to recognize, the genius in the work.

We should reread our own novels-in-progress with a similar goal. We're not all geniuses, we're not all writing masterpieces, but as the first readers of our own work, we should give ourselves the benefit of that hope.

In *The Common Reader*, Virginia Woolf refers to "that gaunt aristocrat, Lady Hester Stanhope, who kept a milk-white horse in her stable in readiness for the Messiah, and was for ever scanning the mountain tops, impatiently but with confidence, for signs of his approach."

It is the simplest advice I can offer: forever scan your own writing in much the same way Lady Hester Stanhope scanned the mountaintops—impatient but confident that a masterpiece might, miraculously, appear.

WILLIAM REHNQUIST, ROBINSON CRUSOE, RABBIT EARS, AND SOMETHING ABOUT PASSION: ADVICE FROM ME TO ME

It's become an interviewing cliché to ask professionals of a certain age what advice they might give their younger selves. My own inclination when asked this question is to say that I wouldn't bother giving advice to my younger self because, having been my younger self, I know I'm the last person I would accept advice from.

But the question does nevertheless inspire some, if not soul-searching, at least autobiography-searching—an opportunity to remember one's younger self as well as the era in which that younger self walked the earth. Nabokov said nostalgia is an "insane companion"; nevertheless, here are a few unrelated, nostalgia-tinged tidbits I might have shared with the young writer I once was, once upon another time.

Justice Rehnquist

By the early 1970s, when I was just graduating from high school, the counterculture shock value of long hair had lost its edge.

Hair, the musical, had opened on Broadway in 1968. In 1970, every high school air guitarist of my acquaintance knew all the words to "Almost Cut My Hair." The late-sixties ideological standoff between men who wore crew cuts and men who let their hair touch their collars had, by the early seventies, abated. Longer hair, longer sideburns went mainstream. You saw it on the men who recited the evening news and the men who hosted TV talk shows, on East and West Coast politicians, even on the nerdiest dads in my neighborhood.

But in my own household, my two college-age brothers (whose hair skimmed their shoulders) and I (whose hair was halfway down my back) threw our hands up in despair every time our father returned from the local barbershop with what was left of his hair trimmed neatly, his sideburns as short as they had been in the thirties and the forties and the fifties. "Come on, Dad," we would argue. "Don't be so old-fashioned."

My father was an Irish Catholic Goldwater Republican who believed in what Faulkner in his Nobel Prize acceptance speech somewhat redundantly called the "old verities and truths," as they were mostly defined by conservatism, Catholicism, Brooks Brothers, and Shakespeare.

We said, "Just let your sideburns grow a little longer. It will make you look younger, more with it."

He said, "To thine own self be true."

We rolled our eyes, of course. It's what our younger selves do.

In 1972, when Richard Nixon, whom my father greatly admired, appointed William Rehnquist to the Supreme Court, I was delighted to find a photograph in the paper that I quickly brandished about the house: Rehnquist had sideburns that reached nearly to his chin.

My father looked at the photo. He grimaced sympathetically. "Years from now," he told me, "you'll look at this picture and feel sorry for the guy. You'll say he was a victim of his times."

When I was in graduate school, all the young women writers wanted to write something political, so that we would be taken seriously, and feminist, because it was a heady time for women everywhere. In an effort to reject the hunting and fishing stories of our professors (this was in New Hampshire), we were reading and imitating literary bestsellers like *The Women's Room*, *Surfacing*, *Memoirs of an Ex–Prom Queen*, *Small Changes*, even *Fear of Flying*. In the years that followed, as we were all scratching out our first novels, the success of Mary Gordon's *Final Payments* or of John Irving's feminist-themed blockbuster, *The World According to Garp*, was very much on our minds.

I began writing my first novel in the basement of the medical library at New York Hospital on Manhattan's Upper East Side, because my husband and I lived a block away and it was a quiet place to work—at least until the Shah of Iran was admitted to the hospital for treatment and riot police and protesters began to gather on York Avenue. I recall that my ambitions at the time were modest: I just wanted to get that first novel written, even if it ended up in a drawer or a wastebasket. I just wanted to see if I could teach myself how it was done.

But if my intentions were modest, they were not necessarily pure: I also wanted to contribute a "You're damn right" to those feminist novels of the seventies. I, too, wanted to make the point that women can be more than wives and mothers; they can have careers, goddammit, they can enjoy sex, eschew romance, escape family obligations, hit the road, grow fur, grow wings.

This was still big news in 1979, as big, as ever-present to our minds, as the Iranian hostage crisis and the shah getting asylum in New York. But, of course, that was then, and when I think of my younger self laboring away to create a female character who would, as one reviewer later put it, "confront us with the eighties" (the 1980s!), I am moved to offer her the same sympathy my father felt for William Rehnquist. She was, alas, a victim of her times.

Advice then, to my younger self: be aware of the temporary within the contemporary. Don't only look *around* for your true subject—not to the day's hot topics, certainly not to the books of the moment, whether they be the feminist tracts of the seventies or the pseudo-Dickensian doorstoppers of the early two thousands; look inward, to the old verities and truths of the human heart, the verities and truths without which, as Faulkner pointed out, any story is ephemeral and doomed.

To thine own self be true has some traction here, despite my own eye-rolling, since it is often the case that young writers who strive to define their moment in time do so not because their particular time moves them, but because they are moved by the personae of other writers who have managed the trick. I, for instance, was never a repressed housewife of the 1960s, but I was gobsmacked by the power and wit and articulateness of the feminist writers of the '70s and wanted to be like them. Think of the influence of the personalities of Hemingway, Kerouac, Plath on various generations of aspiring young writers, or of Jonathan Franzen, David Foster Wallace, Louise Erdrich, or Nell Zink. When I was in grad school, we all wanted to be icy Ann Beattie, wry Rosellen Brown, or witty Margaret Atwood, and imitating their work was one way of taking a stab at being them. It's futile, of course, and, looking back, I might point out to the young writer I was that in many ways learning to recognize one's true subject involves coming to terms with one's true self.

I think of W. B. Yeats:

All my life I have been haunted with the idea that the poet should know all classes of men as one of themselves, that he should combine the greatest possible personal realization with the greatest possible knowledge of the speech and circumstances of the world. Fifteen or twenty years ago I remember longing, with this purpose, to disguise myself as a peasant and wander through the West, and then to ship as sailor. But when one shrinks from all business with a stranger, and with all who are not intimate friends, because one underrates or overrates unknown people, one cannot adventure forth. The artist grows more and more distinct, more and more a being in his own right . . .

Resign yourself to becoming a being, a writer, in your own right, I might advise my younger self, *To thine own self be true*—smug Polonius to all-unheeding Laertes or, more likely, unheeding Ophelia, determined to be drowned.

And speaking of drowning . . .

Robinson Crusoe

In 1980, two years before I published that first novel composed in that basement medical library, I read William Maxwell's *So Long, See You Tomorrow*. It's a beautiful short novel full, by example, of more advice to young writers than any course or lecture can possibly offer. And since my younger self was so taken with the novel, I might use a line of it to offer her advice now, a line that strikes me as particularly pertinent to matters of craft— craft as in both writing and boating. Quoting the Spanish philosopher José Ortega y Gasset, Maxwell's narrator tells us, "Life is, in itself and forever, shipwreck."

I might advise my younger self that my own experience has taught me that at some point in its composition so, too, is every novel: a shipwreck.

No matter how fine the weather the day we set out, no matter how clear and well charted our course as we set sail, there are untold tempests and typhoons ahead, sudden swells, unexpected shoals. You get the metaphor.

In short, what we are confident of when we first conceive of the novel in our heads and, more often than not, in the comfort of our beds, becomes all uncertainty when we face the daily reality of being at our desk, of navigating that tidy vessel of an idea through the practical challenges of what happens on page 50, page 220, page 635; the challenge of discovering, well into the voyage, not only what happens next, but how to say it, how to portray it, how to make it one with what has come before, how to make it matter enough to justify all that will follow.

My much, much younger self—the young reader I was well before I was a young writer—was a sucker for stories about people making do in hard circumstances, from Anne Frank's *Diary of a Young Girl* to Johann David Wyss's *Swiss Family Robinson*, and so I might advise my younger self to consider this shipwreck scene from *Robinson Crusoe*, a book I once loved, as if it were a metaphor for what many of us encounter midway through the composition of a novel.

Let the boat be the work-in-progress; the sea, the pages already written; the shore, the novel's end, or even its publication; the wind, perhaps our own ambition . . .

And now our case was very dismal indeed; for we all saw plainly that the sea went so high that the boat could not live, and that we should be inevitably drowned. As to making sail, we had none, nor if we had could we have done anything with it; so we worked at the oar towards the land, though with heavy hearts, like men going to execution; for we all knew that when the boat came near the shore she would be dashed in a thousand pieces by the breach of the sea. However, we committed our souls to God in the most earnest manner; and with the wind driving us towards the shore, we hastened our destruction with our own hands, pulling as well as we could towards land.

What the shore was, whether rock or sand, whether steep or shoal, we knew not. The only hope that could rationally give us the least shadow of expectation was, if we might find some bay or gulf, or the mouth of some river, where by great chance we might have run our boat in, or got under the lee of the land, and perhaps made smooth water. But there was nothing like this appeared; but as we made nearer and nearer the shore, the land looked more frightful than the sea.

Over the years, I have had some experience with going to my desk every day—pulling toward land, if you will—with a heavy heart, like men going to execution, convinced that I had neither story enough, talent enough, luck enough to get the damn thing completed, that only windy ambition was driving me dangerously on to catastrophe, that I was hastening my destruction with my own hands.

Which may account for why, after that first novel written in the cool confines of the medical library, I developed the habit of working on two novels at once. It's a very bad habit, and I would urge my younger self to avoid it, but, to belabor the seagoing metaphor, it's also a way of reassuring myself that if one novel breaks up against the rocks, there's another sailing just behind . . . a reassuring prospect if you don't consider that Crusoe's doomed ship also had another boat trailing it, for all the good it did him.

We had a boat at our stern just before the storm, but she was first staved by dashing against the ship's rudder, and in the next place she broke away, and either sunk or was driven off to sea; so there was no hope from her.

Looking back, I might advise my younger self that even having two novels-in-progress, or three or four, is no protection against those inevitable moments of abandonment and despair that strike us all in the long haul of composition. Sooner or later the brilliant idea for a novel we set out with will become insufficient to the task—not as clever as we first thought, not as thrilling in execution as it was in fantasy. We have filled pages and pages with words, but the story, or our energy, has run aground. Now what? Here's Robinson Crusoe again:

> . . . I began to look round me, to see what kind of place I was in, and what was next to be done; and I soon found my comforts abate, and that, in a word, I had a dreadful deliverance; for I was wet, had no clothes to shift me, nor anything either to eat or drink to comfort me . . . and this threw me into such terrible agonies of mind, that for a while I ran about like a madman. Night coming upon me, I began with a heavy heart to consider what would be my lot if there were any ravenous beasts in that country, as at night they always come abroad for their prey.
>
> All the remedy that offered to my thoughts at that time was to get up into a thick bushy tree like a fir, but thorny, which grew near me, and where I resolved to sit all night, and consider the next day what death I should die, for as yet I saw no prospect of life.

There's that heavyheartedness again, that heavyheartedness we feel when we look around at the strange place our own writing has delivered us to and realize we have lost control.

Looking back, I might advise my younger self—and save her

from any number of sleepless nights—that loss of control is what we're after.

Because, look, if you have courage enough to sail your novel into the unknown, then you will, inevitably, encounter the unexpected. And if the unexpected is what we hope to find as readers, shouldn't we welcome it as writers, as well? And if welcoming the unexpected means our original scheme for the novel gets swamped, if it means that we look back at what we've written thus far and see no prospect of life in it, fine. Fine. But now a decision must be made.

Will we climb into a bushy tree and wait for the death of this story? Will we hop onto the new boat that is sailing behind, or taking shape in our heads, and leave the wreckage of this one where it is, forever confined to that mythical "drawer" of unpublished and unfinished novels, setting ourselves free from the catastrophe, yes, but also, perhaps, missing out on something wonderful? Consider, for instance, if anyone would know Robinson Crusoe's name had he and his shipmates gotten safely into that second boat.

Or do we salvage what we've got? Revisit those pages that got us here. Reread them with an attentiveness we have, perhaps, not given them before, not as the completed pages of a completed work, but as small sustenance—a detail, a scene, a character, a paragraph, a sentence we can make use of as we explore this newfound land.

Surely there are novels worth abandoning completely, knowing, even as you set off in a brand-new vessel, that shipwreck is once again a possibility. But just as surely there are novels worth salvaging, repurposing in modern jargon, making use of—perhaps even discovering the use of—what you've already established and putting it at the service of what's before you, that is, this new story, new life, this thus far undiscovered, uninhabited island of the novel you didn't know, setting out, you were headed for . . . an undiscovered land in which you may be surprised to find, some fine and lonely day, a footprint in the sand.

But how to judge, my younger self well might ask, when to pursue the story, when to abandon it?

Across the years, I might tell her, she will do both—cut and run on some novels-in-progress and make do with others—and the only criteria she will use, as far as I can determine, are somewhat akin to Robinson Crusoe's: you complete certain novels, you make do with what you've got, simply because you have no choice.

The novel, or perhaps just the characters or the setting or a scene or a sentence, has become, like the poet, a being in its own right, and you must attend to it, be true to it, get on with it, no matter the consequences.

Shakespeare is again pertinent here—bloody Macbeth, not moody Hamlet—a line I've often jotted down, despairingly, in my notebooks in the midst of composition:

> I am in blood
> Stepp'd in so far that, should I wade no more,
> Returning were as tedious as go o'er.

You go o'er because you must, even if you do so like a man going to his execution. Hardly a cheerful prospect for the young writer I once was, but there it is.

And there she goes, I imagine, paying no attention at all.

Rabbit Ears

The farther away my younger self gets, the more I realize how rapidly the taken-for-granted ordinary becomes the antique, the quaint, the comically, astonishingly old-fashioned.

Long ago and far away, before cable and Wi-Fi, when the word *wireless* evoked either Mrs. Miniver's family gathered around a Smart-car-size radio or the "I've Got No Strings" moment in *Pinocchio*, televisions, some may recall, especially what we referred to as "portable televisions," were equipped with antennae—rabbit ears—that could be toyed with and adjusted endlessly.

As I was growing up, most of our television-watching took place in the living room, where the set, as monolithic as the couch, was securely bound to an antenna on the roof. But whenever we went out to the far ends of eastern Long Island for weekends or vacations, we brought the portable. It was here that my younger self observed a significant divide.

For my parents, watching the portable television involved merely turning the thing on, waiting for it to "warm up," giving one or both of the rabbit ears a brief touch of the fingertips to put an end to a rolling line or a peripheral squiggle, and then accepting whatever image arrived, be it blurred or snowy or rolling again, because, after all, we were one hundred miles from Manhattan, and there were only two channels in the Hamptons, and wasn't the fact that a television could be portable and that Walter Cronkite's voice could reach us even out here at the end of the world miracle enough?

My two brothers, however, both of them bound for dual careers as engineers and lawyers, could not be satisfied with anything but a crisp, precise picture. If one of them would leap up to adjust the right ear, the other would insist on fiddling with the left. They would move the rabbit ears to the center of the top of the television, then to either side; then they would see what might happen if they took the rabbit ears off the set altogether, held them up higher, placed them on a chair. They would run to the kitchen for aluminum foil and devise elaborate extensions, flaps, third ears.

"The picture's fine," my parents would insist, meaning simply that they could see it, see something, but my brothers would not be satisfied until they had pulled into the little box a picture that was as clear as anything we had seen on the set at home. As clear as day. My parents would offer astonished praise. We would sit for a minute to admire the clarity of it, and then one or the other of my brothers would leap up to touch the rabbit ears again. I have a distinct memory of a spring-break visit to East Hampton when we watched LBJ's face on the little television as he told the nation he would not run again—a picture so sharp, it was painful to meet the man's eyes.

I might invoke this memory in offering advice to my younger self about suffering over words. There are, speaking broadly, two schools of thought about how to advise young writers in the matter of suffering over words. One says, move on, get it down, get it written, get the broad outlines and shapes of your story onto the page, don't stop, don't let pursuit of perfection paralyze you, shipwreck you (perhaps); worry about clarity later, find the right word later, keep going, keep going. The other says, in the manner of Mark Twain, that since the difference between the right word and the wrong word is the difference between the lightning and the lightning bug, how is one to progress if one does not yet know if what you're after is insects or electricity, an instance of small charm or of large threat, of faeries or of fiery gods?

Journalists and memoirists use words to tell the story of something that has already happened, and for them one word may be as good as another, but fiction writers use words to evoke story out of thin air—the words themselves an incantation, not a report—and so the tale cannot be separated from the words with which it is told.

So suffer, I would advise my younger self. Worry about every word. Everything depends on them.

Here's Susan Sontag from her journals:

Making lists of words, to thicken my active vocabulary. To have puny, not just little, hoax, not just trick, mortifying, not just embarrassing, bogus, not just fake. I could make a story out of puny, hoax, mortifying, bogus. They *are* a story.

Words matter, I would tell my younger self; they're all we've got, and if you're not suffering over every one of them, you're in the wrong profession. Write a blog, not a novel. (Though my young self wouldn't know what a blog is.) Try Twitter, not poetry. (She would think I'd gone word mad.)

Yes, it's true, such suffering over clarity can impede progress, and there are times when you're juggling scene and plot, character, exposition, dialogue, that you have to slap down a wrong word or two just to keep going. But go back as soon as you can. Try to get it right on the next go-through. Try to get it even more right on the next. No musician would justify playing a few wrong notes by saying, I got to the end of the piece, didn't I?

When it comes to words, our one and only tool, there's really no such thing as overthinking things.

Here's Sylvia Townsend Warner writing to William Maxwell, in his capacity as editor, about a story of hers that *The New Yorker* is about to publish:

On galley seven I have substituted clattered for flounced for the noise that Rosalind made with her bucket. If you have a bucket handy, and some nice echoing floor, and snatch the bucket up and put it down again rather violently in much the same place

that you took it up from, that will be what I chose to call flounc-
ing with a bucket, and any one who has taken part in church
decorations, especially at Easter when tempers are at their worse,
will recognize the action; but I daresay some of the New Yorker's
readers only go to quiet things like baseball matches, and so perhaps clattered would be better.

Suffering over words in this way is one of the few pleasures of
our profession. We fiddle with the rabbit ears of every sentence,
not just for precision, meaning, story, but for sound, rhythm, the
beauty of our language.

Recalling that spring night when we watched LBJ on our little portable, I would remind my younger self that without my
brothers' elaborate, and annoying, pursuit of clarity, we might still
have heard the words of the president's address to the nation and
seen the black-and-white outline of his familiar head, but we would
not have noticed the weariness and the sorrow and the unmitigated
pain in the man's eyes. Had the picture remained blurry, or merely
clear enough, my father would not have said when the speech was
over, "He'll be dead in a year once he leaves office."

And it was because of the clarity achieved by my brothers'
fiddling with the rabbit ears, and fiddling again, that none of us
had to ask him what he meant.

But how to choose the right word, my younger self might
ask, whiny and impatient. With so many words to choose from,
with so many ways of saying the same thing, how do you know
when you've got it right, how do you know when to let it stand?

When it's true, I might answer. When the words are honest
and clear and, after tremendous effort, authentically yours. Remember the old verities and truths, my dear, remember *To thine
own self* . . . or, perhaps, I might suggest, it's . . .

Something About Passion

I once taught a class in the short novel in which we read Katherine Anne Porter's *Pale Horse, Pale Rider*. There's a scene toward the end (or toward what might be called the beginning of the end) in which Miranda, just coming down with the Spanish flu—this is Denver in the midst of World War I's flu epidemic—is being cared for by Adam, the young man she has only recently fallen in love with, a young soldier on the verge of being sent overseas.

> He sat on the bed again, dragging up a chair and putting his feet on the rungs. They smiled at each other for the first time since he had come in that night. "How do you feel now?" he asked.
>
> "Better, much better," she told him. "Let's talk. Let's tell each other what we meant to do."
>
> "You tell me first," said Adam. "I want to know about you."
>
> "You'd get the notion I had a very sad life," she said. "And perhaps it was, but I'd be glad enough to have it now. If I could get it back, it would be easy to be happy about almost anything at all. That's not true, but that's the way I feel now." After a pause, she said, "There's nothing to tell, after all, if it ends now, for all this time I was getting ready for something that was going to happen later, when the time came. So now it's nothing much."
>
> "But it must have been worth having until now, wasn't it?" he asked seriously as if it were something important to know.
>
> "Not if this is all," she repeated obstinately.
>
> "Weren't you ever—happy?" asked Adam, and he was

plainly afraid of the word; he was shy of it as he was of the word *love*, he seemed never to have spoken it before, and was uncertain of its sound or meaning.

"I don't know," she said. "I just lived and never thought about it. I remember things I liked, though, and things I hoped for."

"I was going to be an electrical engineer," said Adam. He stopped short. "And I shall finish up when I get back," he added, after a moment.

"Don't you love being alive?" asked Miranda. "Don't you love weather and the colors at different times of the day, and all the noises like children screaming in the next lot, and automobile horns and little bands playing in the street and the smell of food cooking?"

"I love to swim, too," said Adam.

"So do I," said Miranda; "we never did swim together."

In our discussion of the novel, some of my students pointed out that no fiction writer publishing today could possibly write a line of dialogue like, "Don't you love being alive?" They wrinkled their noses. It would just be too much, they said.

Somewhat astonished, I asked them to consider the context— two young people, newly in love, in the midst of a terrible war and a devastating plague, two young people suddenly, vividly, made to face their own mortality.

No, they insisted. (This was years before they would live through their own generation's pandemic.) Even in this context, it was a groan-inducing line for a contemporary reader. Twenty-first-century readers, they informed me, were a cooler, more sophisticated lot, better attuned to falsity, more inclined to irony. They'd know when they were being manipulated for the sake of pathos.

This discussion disturbed me perhaps more than it should

have, made me wonder if I have finally grown too old to offer advice to young writers. Because if coolness and irony are what the contemporary writer and reader are seeking, then I have no advice to give. Remembering my own time in graduate school classes, specifically the graduate school class in which I first read *Pale Horse, Pale Rider*, I recalled how deeply the bitter passion of Porter's story touched me. How I knew intuitively that this was a piece of fiction I would return to again and again throughout my career, just to see how it was done. Just to absorb, if I could, the craft lesson contained therein, which is that the best fiction is a proclamation, in spite of our mortality, in spite of suffering and death and intractable time, of our love for being alive.

Apparently, this was the sort of advice I was willing to take as a young writer, and looking back over the various notebooks I kept then, I discover that it was one with the bits and pieces of writerly advice I jotted down when I was young—all of which, I realize only now, had to do not with what subjects to choose or what drafts to salvage or how to keep those sentences polished, but only with the passion required to enter this profession, and to stay there.

I copied John Steinbeck, for instance:

> If there is a magic in story writing, and I am convinced there is, no one has ever been able to reduce it to a recipe that can be passed from one person to another. The formula seems to lie solely in the aching urge of the writer to convey something he feels important to the reader. If the writer has that urge, he may sometimes, but by no means always, find the way to do it.

I copied this from Annie Dillard:

> Write as if you were dying. At the same time, assume you write for an audience consisting solely of terminal patients. That is,

after all, the case. What would you begin writing if you knew you would die soon? What could you say to a dying person that would not enrage by its triviality?

And the poet Ted Hughes:

In writing you have to distinguish between those things about which you are merely curious . . . and things which are a deep part of your life. You ask yourself: "What can I use next?" You should say: "What can I set on fire next? What genuine interest of mine can I plunge into now and really let myself go? What part of my life would I die to be separated from?"

And here's F. Scott Fitzgerald in a coolly worded letter to a young writer that is also about passion, a letter I copied down, as I recall, during my junior year in college:

Dear Frances,
I've read your story carefully and, Frances, I'm afraid the price for doing professional work is a good deal higher than you are prepared to pay at present.

You've got to sell your heart, your strongest reactions, not the little minor things that only touch you lightly, the little experiences that you might tell at dinner. This is especially true when you begin to write, when you have not yet developed the tricks of interesting people on paper, when you have none of the technique which it takes time to learn. When, in short, you have only your emotions to sell.

This is the experience of all writers. It was necessary for Dickens to put into Oliver Twist the child's passionate resentment at being abused and starved that had haunted his whole childhood. Ernest Hemingway's first stories "In

Our Time" went right down to the bottom of all that he had ever felt and known. In "This Side of Paradise" I wrote about a love affair that was still bleeding as fresh as the skin wound on a haemophile.

. . . the professional, having learned all that he'll ever learn about writing, can take a trivial thing such as the most superficial reactions of three uncharacterized girls and make it witty and charming—the amateur thinks he or she can do the same. But the amateur can only realize his ability to transfer his emotions to another person by some such desperate and radical expedient as tearing your first tragic love story out of your heart and putting it on pages for people to see.

That, anyhow, is the price of admission. Whether you are prepared to pay it or, whether it coincides or conflicts with your attitude on what is "nice" is something for you to decide. But literature, even light literature, will accept nothing less from the neophyte. It is one of those professions that wants the "works." You wouldn't be interested in a soldier who was only a little brave.

In the light of this, it doesn't seem worthwhile to analyze why this story isn't saleable but I am too fond of you to kid you along about it, as one tends to do at my age. If you ever decide to tell your stories, no one would be more interested than,

Your old friend,

F. Scott Fitzgerald

And, of course, there was Faulkner's Nobel Prize acceptance speech. A speech that the young writer I once was—donning oversized earphones and knowing just where to place the needle on the revolving 78—listened to over and over again on many a snowy day in the very high-tech, very modern "audio room" of the library at Oswego State, in that other country that is the past:

> Our tragedy today is a general and universal physical fear so long sustained by now that we can even bear it. There are no longer problems of the spirit. There is only the question: When will I be blown up? Because of this, the young man or woman writing today has forgotten the problems of the human heart in conflict with itself which alone can make good writing because only that is worth writing about, worth the agony and the sweat.
>
> He must learn them again. He must teach himself that the basest of all things is to be afraid; and, teaching himself that, forget it forever, leaving no room in his workshop for anything but the old verities and truths of the heart, the old universal truths lacking which any story is ephemeral and doomed—love and honor and pity and pride and compassion and sacrifice. Until he does so, he labors under a curse. He writes not of love but of lust, of defeats in which nobody loses anything of value, of victories without hope and, worst of all, without pity or compassion. His griefs grieve on no universal bones, leaving no scars. He writes not of the heart but of the glands.
>
> Until he relearns these things, he will write as though he stood among and watched the end of man. I decline to accept the end of man. It is easy enough to say that man is immortal simply because he will endure: that when the last dingdong of doom has clanged and faded from the last worthless rock hanging tideless in the last red and dying evening, that even then there will still be one more sound: that of his puny inexhaustible voice, still talking.
>
> I refuse to accept this. I believe that man will not merely endure: he will prevail. He is immortal, not because he alone among creatures has an inexhaustible voice, but because he has a

soul, a spirit capable of compassion and sacrifice and endurance. The poet's, the writer's, duty is to write about these things. It is his privilege to help man endure by lifting his heart, by reminding him of the courage and honor and hope and pride and compassion and pity and sacrifice which have been the glory of his past. The poet's voice need not merely be the record of man, it can be one of the props, the pillars to help him endure and prevail.

What advice would I offer my younger self? None. What would be the use?

She's busy listening to Faulkner with those big headphones on, or she's exiled herself to the basement library of the medical school. Or she's heading for her desk like a man to his execution, or obsessively fiddling with those damn words. She's stuck in the perpetual adolescence of the forever aspiring; she's a starry-eyed romantic, except when she's a terrified realist; she's stubborn, impractical, full of hope, full of despair . . . full of passion for the task at hand, which is simply to ask, through stories that admit of death and disappointment and sorrow and loss, Don't you just love life?

She wants to be a writer, poor dear.

There's no use, finally, in trying to tell her anything at all.

AN UNREASONABLE DEGREE OF SYMPATHY

I was introduced to the work of Stig Dagerman by his daughter, Lo. At the time we were both mothers of preschool sons, and in the way of mothers overseeing playdates, we had begun to exchange brief biographies as we sat together on Lo's back deck while our boys played their imaginary games in her leafy backyard. I learned that Lo's father had been a Swedish writer of much renown—a novelist, a short-story writer, a poet, and a playwright. He was also a journalist. In 1946, he had been sent on assignment to postwar Germany to record the devastation there, one of the first independent journalists to do so. His second wife, Lo's mother, Anita Björk, was an actress. He died by suicide in 1954, at age thirty-one, when Lo was younger than our sons were now.

Of course, I asked if her father's work was available in English. Lo had a British edition of *German Autumn*, her father's collected articles about the German people after the fall of the Third Reich; a book of short stories called *The Games of Night*; and a novel, *A Burnt Child*. She hoped eventually, she said, to find some time (as working mothers of preschool children, we were well familiar with that *how to find the time* refrain) to seek out an American translator for her father's work.

Our four-year-olds were running and calling in the yard. A suburban autumn, as I recall. It so happened, I told her, that among my graduate students that semester was a very bright and talented young fiction writer named Steven Hartman who was also fluent in Swedish.

It's inevitable, perhaps, that while reading Steven Hartman's translations of Stig Dagerman's stories collected in *Sleet*, I found myself recalling something of the substance of those days when Lo and I were young mothers standing watchful on the periphery of our small sons' games. Young boys, after all, imaginative young boys, appear often enough in these stories: large-eyed, as one thinks of them, tentative, observant, loving, lonely. And I suppose it could be argued that the various autobiographical settings of the stories—from the small farms and villages (Dagerman himself spent his first six years living on his grandparents' farm in Alvkarleby) to the working-class flats of Stockholm (where he later lived with his father and stepmother)—have a kind of parallel in that urban-rural convergence that is a secluded backyard in a busy American suburb.

But personal experience and its attendant associations seem insufficient to explain the depth of feeling that these stories achieve. For me, there is something at work here that calls to mind much more than the circumstances of my own introduction to Dagerman's writing. It is, I think, a tremendous generosity of heart, an overwhelming empathy expressed in tandem with a keen awareness of the inevitable suffering, the loneliness and pain, the pettiness and cruelty, that make up the human experience.

There is a compassion to Dagerman's clear-eyed vision of the world that causes me to recall as I read these stories not merely the circumstances that brought me to his work, but the less tangible experience of being a young mother watching over a young child's play: that heady mix of caution, joy, pride, fear, helplessness, and love.

I confess that this was not what I expected to find from this tragic Swedish writer when I opened *German Autumn*, the first of his works I borrowed from his daughter. I expected darkness. Angst. The void. Hopelessness. What I found instead was an account of human suffering unbiased by politics or nationalism, hatred or revenge. An account of human suffering given with both a novelist's eye ("A big bare room with a cement floor and a window that has been almost entirely bricked up. A solitary bulb hangs from the ceiling and shines unmercifully on three air-raid-shelter beds, a stove reeking with sour wood, a small woman with a chalk-white face stirring a pot on the stove, a small boy lying on the bed and staring up apathetically at the light") and a humanitarian's "respect for the individual even when the individual has forfeited our sympathy and compassion . . . the capacity to react in the face of suffering whether that suffering may be deserved or undeserved."

Dagerman writes:

> People hear voices saying that things were better before [Hitler's defeat], but they isolate these voices from the circumstances in which their owners find themselves and they listen to them in the same way as we listen to voices on the radio. They call this objectivity because they lack the imagination to visualize these circumstances and indeed, on the grounds of moral decency, they would reject such an imagination because it would appeal to an unreasonable degree of sympathy. People analyze: in fact it is a kind of blackmail to analyze the political leanings of the hungry without at the same time analyzing hunger.

An imagination that appeals to an unreasonable degree of sympathy is precisely what makes Dagerman's fiction so evocative. Evocative not, as one might expect, of despair or bleakness or existential angst, but of compassion, fellow-feeling, even love. The brief story "To Kill a Child," as unsparing as it is—"Because life is constructed in such a merciless fashion, even one minute before a cheerful man kills a child he can still feel entirely at ease"—ends up being a lament, not a shrug; a lament for all of us at the mercy of merciless time, unwitting victims of life's circumstances.

Dagerman rivals Joyce in his ability to depict the intractable loneliness of childhood, but time and again, in stories like "The Surprise," "The Games of Night," and the marvelous "Sleet," he tempers this loneliness with brief gestures of hope, connectedness: the poem on the phonograph record, the bright coins from a father's drinking companions, the warm hand of the aunt from America. There are tears in these stories, for sure, cruelties, eruptions of violence, but none of this is offered without pity, and even in his stories in which irony reigns—"Men of Character," "Bon Soir"—Dagerman never turns a cold eye on his creations.

Greta in "Bon Soir," a ship's dishwasher with teeth that "look like they're covered in cement, sweating cement," has propositioned Sune, the story's fifteen-year-old protagonist. He is repulsed by her but also charmed by the thought of a woman waiting for him in one of the ship's cabins. And then, while the boat is docked, he sees her being led away by two detectives; he later learns she has been spreading venereal disease in the port.

> As he approaches the gangplank, Sune notices something peculiar and disquieting. Paul and the drunken first mate and several others are just standing around on the foredeck, idly waiting for something. And now the door swings open, and out steps

the small, slender man in the trench coat. He turns and holds the door for Greta, as the large, heavyset man with the cigar clenched between his teeth walks directly behind her with a small, shabby suitcase in his right hand. In single file they walk up the foredeck gangplank, and suddenly Greta spots him there. She looks up at him hastily, and later he will think back on that look many times—something impossible to forget.

"Bon soir," she says and almost drops her handbag. "Bon soir." And that's when he notices she is crying.

Life may be merciless, but the creator of this scene—who notes Greta's shabby suitcase, her hasty look, her pitiful "bon soir," her fumbled handbag, her tears—is not.

The long last story in Steven Hartman's translation, "Where Is My Icelandic Sweater," is both a comic masterpiece and a heartbreaking depiction of degradation and loneliness. Knut is a bore, a drunk, a braggart, and yet even as the reader is absorbed into his careening and very funny interior monologue of self-righteousness, self-pity, self-delusion, we are given opportunity to recognize, too, the very human longing at the heart of his nature. Like the cheerful man in "To Kill a Child," what Knut wants is a simple impossibility: to gain back a single minute of his life.

Here on the old man's couch, stripped pretty much naked, blubbering . . . And this is where we sat, me and him, the last time we ever saw each other . . . this is right where the old man put his arm around me and gave me a big squeeze. And then he got up and went over to that dresser there and rummaged around in the drawer for something. After a while he got his hands on what he was after and he laid it out right here on the table. A little sweater.

"'Member this, Knut?" he said to me. "'Member this Icelandic sweater? I picked it up for you one Christmas in the city.
And you, well, I ain't never seen a kid so goddamned pleased
with anything in my life . . ."

I could do with that Icelandic sweater right about now.
The old man, he had it in his hands the last time I was here. I
sure could do with it, alright, to hold under the blanket whiles
I think about the old man.

There is much tenderness in this moment, as there is in every
Dagerman story, a tenderness that does not seek to distract the
reader from what is terrible about human experience, but man-
ages instead to confirm it. Were it not for such tenderness, after
all, cruelty would be of no matter. Were it not for those fleeting
moments of connection, loneliness would not sting. Without an
imagination that appeals to an unreasonable degree of sympathy,
human suffering—the suffering of the likes of Knut and Greta,
or of the people of Germany after the Second World War—
would be met with no more than the skimming indifference we
afford the inevitable, or dismissed as no less than what some of
us deserve.

Stig Dagerman possessed just such an imagination. No
doubt it caused him much pain. But as his stories prove, there
is redemption in such an unreasonable degree of sympathy: by
its grace, by the grace of the artist who wields it, tenderness survives, fellow-feeling; the mercy that merciless life itself does not
provide survives, the mercy we might still offer to one another,
in joy and fear and helplessness and love.

STARTING OVER

I had only one novel and a sprinkling of short stories on my résumé when I was given the precarious title of writer-in-residence by the English department of a small Southern college and stationed there for six weeks one autumn to teach and advise undergraduate writers who were no more sure of what they were doing than I was.

For sustenance during those damp and lonely days when the residing was going far better than the writing, I bought a paperback copy of *Middlemarch* at the college bookstore. I had the idea that throughout my career as a writer I would revisit every novel I had loved thus far, every novel that I could, perhaps—depending on how it all turned out—blame or praise for having gotten me into this business in the first place.

Middlemarch, I knew, was surely one of these: a book that got me into this business, a book I had loved as an undergraduate myself, that I could now reread, not as I had read it first, as a vague English major at a state college on the frozen shores of Lake Ontario, but as a fellow writer, a published novelist—even, for these six weeks, a *Southern* novelist—a writer-in-residence with a novel-in-progress. A well-hyphenated professional.

I was at the time far into, as we say, my second novel. It was the story of an ordinary couple in an ordinary suburb whose small child is stricken with a peculiar disease that suddenly transforms their lives into the stuff of soap opera and maudlin human-interest journalism. My editor had already read the first hundred pages or so and been properly enthusiastic, and I had a contract with my publisher that said I would deliver the book by the end of the year.

I had planned, then, to be totally focused and productive during my six weeks alone (my husband was back in New York) in my little college-provided writer's cottage. I knew what I had to write and what I was going to write. Now I would simply write it.

But in my first few days in my idyllic abode, I discovered I couldn't. I mean, I could, I could write, but I didn't. Well, actually, I did. I wrote every day, but—more pertinent—I didn't want to. I'd had one novel that was reviewed kindly in a weekday edition of *The New York Times* and on the front page of a Sunday's *New York Times Book Review*, where I was called an emerging writer, and now I was feeling timid about what would come next, once I'd emerged. I was feeling timid but also uninspired. Also lazy. Wary. Unsure.

So that October night when I curled up with *Middlemarch* in my narrow writer-in-residence bed in my dark little writer-in-residence residence, I was immediately surprised and delighted to find exactly what I was looking for. Right there, in the brief prelude that begins the novel, was the inspiration I required: a reiteration of the very themes I had hoped to develop in my own work, the very ideas that had gotten me started in this profession in the first place:

Who that cares much to know the history of man, and how the mysterious mixture behaves under the varying experiments

of Time, has not dwelt, at least briefly, on the life of Saint Theresa, has not smiled with some gentleness at the thought of the
little girl walking forth one morning hand in hand with her
still smaller brother to go and seek martyrdom in the country
of the Moors? Out they toddled from rugged Avila, wide-eyed
and helpless-looking as two fawns, but with human hearts,
already beating to a national idea; until domestic reality met
them in the shape of uncles and turned them back from their
great resolve. That childhood pilgrimage was a fit beginning.
Theresa's passionate, ideal nature demanded an epic life . . .

That Spanish woman who lived three hundred years ago
was certainly not the last of her kind. Many Theresas have
been born who found for themselves no epic life wherein there
was a constant unfolding of far-resonant action: perhaps only
a life of mistakes, the offspring of a certain spiritual grandeur ill-matched with the meanness of opportunity; perhaps
a tragic failure which found no sacred poet and sank unwept
into oblivion . . .

Here and there is born a Saint Theresa, foundress of nothing, whose loving heartbeats and sobs after an unattained
goodness tremble off and are dispersed among hindrances instead of centering in some long-recognizable deed.

This was the inspiration, the encouragement, I needed. Weren't
the women in my own novel just such Theresas? Wasn't the irony
of my novel-in-progress born of the notion that they, too, would
have missed the opportunity for spiritual grandeur, an epic life,
had it not come to them, all unbidden, in the form of their
child's cruel and devastating illness?

George Eliot's words assured me of this much: I had an intention, of sorts, as vague as it was compelling. I wanted to write
about these women, these Saint Theresas who longed for but

missed the epic life, who were foundresses of nothing. I wanted
to say something about them. I didn't yet know what that something was, but Eliot's words reminded me that I actually had
ideas about my own characters. I actually had my own characters. I had intentions. I had, by God, themes.

I also had that fall a student in my writing workshop who
claimed that his life—if not yet his fiction—also had themes.
When Bob would arrive late for a conference, disheveled and
only half awake, the folds of his pillow still marking his unshaven
cheek, he would say in his gentle Tidewater way, "See, this is one
of my themes: sleep is important." Or when an assignment was
late or only half completed: "One of my themes is to give everything its own time." Other students had scheduling conflicts or
impacted wisdom teeth or emotional crises; Bob had themes.

There were dormitories lining the street just across from my cottage, and that night as I sought inspiration from *Middlemarch*,
I was vaguely aware of the voices of drunken undergraduates
calling out to one another. I recognized the lines from an Eddie
Murphy routine that had recently aired on HBO, a raunchy riff
on the old *Honeymooners* sitcom in which, the premise went,
Ralph and Norton were gay.

As I eased myself back into the life of Dorothea Brooke, I
heard that routine's obscene refrain repeated and repeated and
repeated by these raucous undergrads: *Hey, Norton, how would
you like to . . .* Followed again and again by gales of cackling
laughter.

But this was not the thing that made me close the book on
that October evening.

It was rather that as I read, I found myself seized with a bitter, nearly unbearable envy.

George Eliot, it occurred to me, was not only brilliant and clever and funny and wise, a marvelous, marvelous writer, a genius, but she was also finished. Finished writing. Her work was done. It was incredible work: *Adam Bede*, *The Mill on the Floss*, *Silas Marner*, and this *Middlemarch*, masterpieces all; but far more enviable to me on that damp Southern night, with only one novel published and a second grinding to a halt, was that her work was finished. Over. No more rewrites or revisions for George Eliot. No more of that sinking feeling at chapter 3 (or 18) that this was not really the story you wanted to tell, not really the voice you wanted to use. No more elaborate justifications for the hours you've spent, a regular Flaubert, searching for just the right verb to use in this perfect description of a meaningful gesture made by an incredibly endearing character who happens to be the protagonist of an ill-conceived scene that finally just doesn't belong.

No more reluctantly admitting to yourself, just when you were hoping to walk away, close up shop, close the computer, open a beer, that yes, this paragraph, this scene, this chapter, this sentence, this plot, could be better. No more late-night realizations that although you seemed, miraculously, to have entered, or at least crossed the threshold of, the exalted profession you longed to join, although you were, indeed, a writer-in-residence with a novel-in-progress, you were not, in fact ("Hey, Norton!"), absolutely not ("How would *you* like to . . ."), having any fun at all.

I think of Philip Roth's E. I. Lonoff, the Great Writer in *The Ghost Writer*:

> "I turn sentences around. That's my life. I write a sentence and
> then I turn it around. Then I look at it and I turn it around
> again. Then I have lunch. Then I come back in and write an-
> other sentence. Then I have tea and turn the new sentence

around. Then I read the two sentences over and turn them both around. Then I lie down on my sofa and think. Then I get up and throw them out and start from the beginning."

Or Willem de Kooning's reply to Elaine Benson when she asked why he'd never been to Las Vegas:

You see, I'm a painter. And the trouble is, if you're a painter, you get up in the morning and you work for a while. Then you have something to eat. And then you go back to work. You stop and you worry about what you are doing. And you work some more. Then you stop and have something to eat. Then you're tired, so you watch some TV. Then you go to bed, but you worry about what you did in your work that day. So you get up and you work some more. Then you go back to bed and you worry . . . So on what day would I go to Las Vegas?

George Eliot was through with all that. Her novels were complete. Her work was done. She would never again have to worry, turn a sentence around, throw it out, rewrite it, rewrite it again, start over. She was finished. The fact that she was also dead offered little consolation that October night in the narrow bedroom of my tiny writer's residence. I wanted my work to be finished, too. And it wasn't. Not even close.

At the college that semester, there was another visitor, a British professor, a brilliant critic, I was told, author of many acclaimed books of superior scholarship, the kind of academic seldom found at obscure little liberal arts colleges such as this one, and here only because he had come to the region for a short sabbatical and had met and married a local girl. I could tell he intimidated everyone else in the English department, what with his credentials and his accent and his noblesse oblige. But he was most gracious to me on our first meeting, implying in his graciousness that we were both of a larger and far more interesting world than the one inhabited by our country-bumpkin colleagues. When he asked me in the hallway one afternoon what I was reading—"Besides," he said, indicating the student manuscripts I held in my arms, "this drivel"—I told him that I was rereading *Middlemarch* but having a tough time of it, envious as I was that Eliot had finished her masterwork, gotten through the last draft.

He looked down at me along his narrow, House of Lords nose. "Yes," he said, "but some writers require more drafts than others, don't they?"

Don't you? was clearly implied.

It was not that I didn't want to write. I was, as I said, writing every day. It was more that I didn't want to write the story I was bound to, the story I had already spent a good year with, the story my editor had read and my publisher had paid me for. It was a decent story, I supposed. Carefully wrought—so far anyway—populated with strong characters. A serious story not without humor. And I was pretty sure I knew just how it was supposed to turn out.

I just didn't want to write it.

I had only done this novel thing once before (not counting the novel I had written when I was twelve, when the niceties of composition were lost on me entirely and the pathway from head to paper was immediate and direct), but I had enough experience as a writer by then to know that it was only a matter of waiting this out, this curious writer's block, writing through my own reluctance to continue. Sticking with it.

Somewhere in my notebooks I had scribbled W. H. Auden's words from *The Dyer's Hand and Other Essays*:

> The degree of excitement which a writer feels during the process of composition is as much an indication of the value of the final result as the excitement felt by a worshiper is an indication of the value of his devotions, that is to say, very little indication.

I had, after all, a contract, nearly two hundred pages, and an opportunity to be finished—at least with this one. Finished. Open a beer. Bring on the art director, the book tour, the reviews and interviews—the fun stuff. If I could just stick with this damn novel a little longer, it would be finished. The only problem was, of course, that I wanted it to be finished more than I wanted to write it.

In the years since, I have come to understand that this is not an uncommon dilemma. I see traces of it in the aspiring writers who ask me if they should send a synopsis of their novel to a literary agent well before they have written the first word. I hear it in the *How many pages before* category of inquiry I get from readers who want to be writers: How many pages must I write before I get an agent, an editor, a contract? I see it in the impatient ambition of undergraduates who want to have a novel ready to send out by graduation, or before they apply to medical school. In the *You've got to be kidding* stares of graduate students when they slide a thick manuscript across my desk and I slide it back to them a week later with the suggestion that the story needs a different approach. I hear it in the stunned silence of first-novelist friends who tell me their book is off to the printer, so what should they do now: hire a PR firm? track print runs? increase their online presence? make advertising demands? perhaps devise their own book tour? To which I can only reply, simply, "Now you should write another."

I once told a class of third graders that to be a writer was to have homework due for the rest of your life, and the groans were deafening. What about after you finish a book? one of them asked. "You're never finished, kid," I growled.

With the undergraduates continuing to whoop it up outside my window, not doing their homework either, I found my-self avoiding my writing desk in favor of the kitchen table, and rather than working out the narrative lines of my well-considered themes about epic longings in obscure lives, I wrote instead a scene that had nothing at all to do with the novel thus far, a scene that also had teenagers in it, a summer night, voices calling loudly, plaintively (not, as it turned out, "Hey, Norton!") across a quiet summer lawn that was located somewhere between imagination and memory. It was fun but a little dangerous. This, I knew, was not the way to get my book finished by the end of the year.

Bob, my student who lived by his themes, walked into my office one morning and threw himself, disconsolate, into a chair. "I have to drop my math class," he said. "It's an eight-thirty class, and getting up that early is messing up my whole system. I have to drop it."

Although Bob was a second-semester senior, he'd already been an undergraduate at the school for nine years. So I felt, on his behalf, somewhat dismayed.

"But, Bob," I said, "if you drop your math class, you won't be able to graduate."

He slowly looked up at me. Shaking off his own despair, he smiled with a kind of dawning sympathy, clearly trying to make allowance for the fact that I was, as he liked to say, "one of those New Yorkers," meaning one of those impatient, overly ambitious, shortsighted types.

"Average life expectancy for a male," he drawled, "is seventy-four. I'm only twenty-nine. I'll graduate."

I admitted nothing, not even to myself. The book my editor was waiting for, the book I'd promised, the book with all the heady themes and rich ironies would, I was certain, eventually be finished, but in the meantime there was this other thing I was writing, furtively, furtively, furtively enjoying my own disobedience, my own procrastination, the secret writing life behind the writing life of the writer-in-residence.

I was, I knew, setting myself adrift and that the moment of finishing had now receded beyond the horizon—may even have disappeared altogether—but I was, once again, enjoying the journey out, the writing, the laying down of one sentence after the other, then turning them around, then lying down to worry about them, and then getting up to work on them again.

On my desk were nearly two hundred pages of a story I knew all too well—its themes, its ironies, its plot and characters. On my kitchen table, a story I was only beginning to learn, that was revealing itself slowly, as any good story is revealed to a reader, word by word by word. One felt like homework. The other, guilty pleasure. One already had its assigned themes. The other was a mystery.

The provost at the college hosted an open house one afternoon to show off his newly restored antebellum mansion. The house itself was lovely, but the decorator, who was also the provost's younger wife, had a predilection for tulle and lace and shades of violet. In fact, she and her husband, who greeted everyone graciously at the door, were dressed in variations on the home's color scheme. As I made my way through the rooms, I ran into Bob, who was standing in the doorway of a small, fuchsia-colored sitting room, looking mildly amused. "Some house," I said. Bob shook his head. "Man of a certain age puts on a purple shirt," he whispered, "you know it ain't his own idea."

There was another item I had copied from Auden's book:

No writer can ever judge exactly how good or bad a work of his may be, but he can always know, not immediately perhaps, but certainly in a short while, whether something he has written is authentic—in his handwriting—or a forgery.

When my older son was in high school, he was taught by a legendary English teacher. Mr. Cannon required that all first drafts and all revisions be written by hand. He required that his young writers begin each assignment with what he called "spillage"—a page filled with notes and phrases and ideas about the assigned theme, a free-flowing setting down of thoughts and possibilities, a spontaneous mess of words unencumbered by what Mr. Cannon called the Peanut Man, that cautious, internal editor who shouts warnings from the peanut gallery of the mind. Then, three drafts written at twenty-four-hour intervals. The first two, he told his students, should be a mess, as well: crossed out, written over. These two drafts Mr. Cannon read and returned, words circled and underlined, the first page stamped with his own special stamp that said YOU FREQUENTLY VIOLATE THESE RULES and then listed his own ten rules for good writing:

Write to express, not to impress.
Be proud of what you write.

Rewrite always.
Limit forms of the verb "to be."
Choose the exact word.
Avoid clichés.
Use cautiously simile, metaphor, and personification.
Set inanimate objects against one another.
Vary sentence structure.
Create transitions.
Proof your clean copy.

If a rule was checked, then the student knew what to do in the next rewrite—which was also meant to be done in three drafts, written at twenty-four-hour intervals, all corrections made by hand.

It was rule three, *Rewrite always*, that gave my son the most trouble, and it prompted Mr. Cannon to write him this wonderful note:

> You seem to be insisting on the old "make changes as you re-copy" kind of revision. I think you are still listening to the Peanut Man who says, "Save time, save time." This hurts your writing, because the changes you make under his direction are only briefly considered, possibly even more haphazard than your original spillage. True revision is a taking hold, a honing and a shaping. Please get rid of this Peanut Man and his bad advice. Rather than save time, I want you to spend it. The Peanut Man is not speeding you up; he's slowing you down, and you've got a voice to catch.

No doubt the Peanut Man has whispered in the ear of many of us when we discover that we want our novels to be finished more than we want to write them. Revision is indeed a honing and a shaping, a taking hold, writing a sentence and turning it around, even starting over. Revision is laconically telling the Peanut Man when he whispers, *Finish it, finish it,* "Average life expectancy for a writer is . . . I'll finish it."

Some years after my time as writer-in-residence, after that furtive, not-supposed-to-be-writing-this story had been published as my second novel, I looked again at those abandoned two hundred pages. I recognized then that the story, as complex as I'd intended, with lovable characters and some nice scenes, some pretty lines, was, in effect, a situation tragedy that could not evolve beyond its own premise—a young and self-consciously literary writer's equivalent of that Eddie Murphy routine, you know, *What if Ralph and Norton were gay*—a premise that could play itself out only through repetition, more of the same, the same raucous laughter, the same sad irony. It was, I saw, a prisoner of its own initial ideas, its own heady themes. It wasn't bad, but it wasn't, alas, authentic—in my own hand.

Of course, nothing is ever lost, or so we tell ourselves, and I don't think it hurts us to believe it. Nearly twenty years later, I found a young female character who was, perhaps, "the offspring of a certain spiritual grandeur ill-matched with the meanness of opportunity," a character I named Theresa. Fifteen years more and I had written a novel that, it might be said, is indeed about women "whose loving heartbeats and sobs after an unattained goodness tremble off and are dispersed . . ."

Just before I left the college that fall with fifty pages of a new work and the burden of breaking the news to my ever-patient agent and editor—they both said, quite amicably, "Fine. You know what you're doing" (Ha!)—the administration decided that it was time to reward its generous and no doubt prestige-starved British professor with a Distinguished Teaching Award. There would be a ceremony in the spring, a formal citation, articles in the local press. When an English department secretary called the professor's former university in the United Kingdom, seeking to confirm the accuracy of his long list of publications, her counterpart in England said, "Wait a minute, he just walked in. I'll put him on and he can tell you himself."

It turned out that this slumming academic—in an act of revision that made my own seem paltry and thin—had borrowed the name and the biography and the distinguished list of publications from the original item, who was still very much a British literary scholar living in Britain.

Those of us who tell stories have no choice but to admire the man. For clearly, he understood, as all of us who write fiction sooner or later understand, that sometimes nothing short of starting over will do.

COACHING

I picked up Leo Tolstoy's treatise *What Is Art?* because I was going to Florence and wanted to remember what he'd had to say about religious painting.

I had read sections of his long essay years ago, in graduate school, where it was assigned along with Forster's *Aspects of the Novel* in what I saw in retrospect as a good-cop, bad-cop ploy on the part of my professor: Forster the shuffling good cop, urging us gently, self-effacingly, to think a little harder about what we expect of the novel ("Yes, oh, dear, yes, the novel tells a story"); Tolstoy the Russian graybeard calling us practitioners of "counterfeit art" should we claim beauty or pleasure as our goal or fail to see that art is quite simply one of the conditions of human life, a condition indispensable to its progress.

According to the grumbling Tolstoy, three evils cooperate to result in the production of counterfeit art: "(1) the considerable remuneration of artists for their productions, (2) art criticism, (3) schools of art."

Reading his essay this time around, I had no trouble agreeing with him about the detrimental effect of the considerable remuneration of artists (most of the real writers I know have not been much corrupted by such a circumstance), and I laughed wickedly along with him when he quoted a friend who defined the relationship of critics and artists as "the stupid discussing the wise."

But I must admit I blanched a little when I got to his dismissal of schools of art, since my very reason for going to Italy, the very occasion for rereading his book, was, in fact, to lead a summer writing workshop.

Here is Tolstoy the bad cop on the idea that art can be taught in schools—or, by implication, at summer writing workshops:

"In these schools," he writes in high dudgeon, "art is taught! But art is the transmission to others of a special feeling experienced by the artist. How can this be taught in schools?"

"No school," he goes on to say, "can evoke feeling in a man, and still less can it teach him how to manifest it in the one particular manner natural to him alone. But the essence of art lies in these things.

"The one thing these schools can teach is how to transmit feelings experienced by other artists in the way those other artists transmitted them."

"In literary art," he writes, indignation in every syllable, "people are taught how, without having anything they wish to say, to write a many-paged composition on a theme about which they have never thought, and moreover, to write it so that it should resemble the work of an author admitted to be celebrated. This is taught in schools."

Rereading Tolstoy's essay after all these years—years spent in universities and at writers' workshops teaching people how to write many-paged stories (a good number of them based on themes about which the author had never thought) and doing so precisely by offering as models the work of authors admitted to be celebrated—I was nevertheless pleased to discover that, rather than cringing in shame under the Russian bad cop's glowering stare or simply throwing the book across the room in my own curmudgeonly disagreement, I found myself thinking that Leo Tolstoy would have made a great workshop leader.

Sorry, Leo.

In his introductory remarks in *Aspects of the Novel*, Forster gently tells us that "the final test of a novel will be our affection for it, as it is the test of our friends and of anything else which we cannot define."

A true and lovely sentiment, I think, but a disastrous approach for a group of aspiring writers gathered in a workshop. Disastrous because it will set loose in that environment the worst of all possible conversations, the ones that begin, "Well, I liked it," and end in that blind alley of "Who's to say what's good or bad if people like it?"

But Tolstoy as workshop leader would have no qualms about claiming the authority to say what makes a piece of literature a work of art.

"The activity of art," he writes, "is based on the fact that a man, receiving through his sense of hearing or sight another man's expression of feeling, is capable of experiencing the emotion which moved the man who expressed it. To take the simplest example: one man laughs, and another, who hears, becomes merry, or a man weeps, and another, who hears, feels sorrow.

"It is on this capacity of man to receive another man's expression of feeling, and experience those feelings himself, that the activity of art is based."

Art, Tolstoy writes, "begins when one person, with the object of joining another or others to himself in one and the same feeling, expresses that feeling by certain external indications . . . To invoke in oneself a feeling one has once experienced, and having evoked it in oneself, then, by means of movements, lines and colors, sounds, or forms expressed in words, so to transmit that feeling that others may experience the same feeling—this is the activity of art."

"There is one indubitable indication distinguishing real art from its counterfeit," he goes on to say, "namely, the infectiousness of art."

What a tough, marvelous criterion to use in considering one another's work. *Infection.* The word's biological implications alone can give us a new way to look at the stories brought to a writing workshop: I have been infected by your work. It has entered my bloodstream, overcome my resistance. It has made your fever, your pain, your delirium, my own.

So while Forster might begin a workshop discussion by asking, "How much affection do you have for this piece before us?" Tolstoy will ask, "Has it infected you?"

The stakes, you might say, are raised.

Tolstoy then goes on to demolish another bane of the writing workshop experience, perhaps of the writing profession itself— the soul-sucking notion of literary competition:

> The chief peculiarity of this feeling [infectiousness] is that the receiver of a true impression is so united with the artist that he feels as if the work were his own and not someone else's—as if what it expresses were just what he had long been wishing to express.

That mealymouthed reader's response "I liked it" or "I thought it was interesting" is replaced by this cry from the heart: "I feel I have written it myself." The very notion of competition becomes nonsensical, then, in light of that kind of satisfaction and gratitude: Yes, this is what I've been longing to say / to hear / to read; who cares where it came from, who wrote it, whether it's yours or mine—here it is!

And there's more. With Tolstoy as our workshop leader, all unhelpful talk of affection for a piece of fiction because I see myself in it—or my ancestors, or my culture, my sexual preferences, my neighborhood, my adolescence, my politics—is banished, as well.

> A real work of art destroys, in the consciousness of the receiver, the separation between himself and the artist, nor that alone, but also between himself and all whose minds receive this work of art. In this freeing of our personality from its separation and isolation, in this uniting of it with others, lies the chief characteristic and the great attractive force of art.

Flaubert famously said, "Madame Bovary, c'est moi," but the triumph of any great novel's artistry, Tolstoy claims, is that the reader is moved to say the same. I am Madame Bovary. I am Elizabeth Bennet. I am Hazel Motes or Washington Black or Ethan Frome or Annie John or Thérèse Raquin or Okonkwo. I am freed from the human condition of separation and isolation: I am another.

As the leader of our writing workshop, Tolstoy also provides our discussions with a means of determining not only if we have been infected by a work of art (caught the fever) but the degree to which we have been infected (how high?).

"The degree of infectiousness in art," Tolstoy tells us, "depends on three conditions":

1. on the greater or lesser individuality of the feeling transmitted;
2. on the greater or lesser clearness with which the feeling is transmitted;

3. on the sincerity of the artist; i.e., on the greater or lesser force with which the artist himself feels the emotion he transmits.

Individuality, clarity, sincerity. Three marvelous criteria by which to view the works-in-progress we bring to our own "art schools."

And yet, even as it occurs to me that Tolstoy would run a pretty tight classroom, I also see the glare of the man's keen, interrogatory indignation:

How, he will ask, can any of this be taught in schools?

Individuality?

"The more individual the feeling, the more strongly does it act on the receiver; the more individual the state of soul into which he is transferred, the more pleasure does the receiver obtain, and therefore the more readily and strongly does he join in it."

Surely none of us would write fiction if we did not believe in the individuality of each and every human creature—or, at the least, the particularly impressive individuality that is ours, or our characters', alone. If we did not value the unique state of the soul of every fictional character, whether Molly Bloom or Rabbit Angstrom, Becky Sharp, Jean Brodie, or Count Pierre Kirillovich Bezukhov, we would not seek to make individual and unique the characters of our own imaginations. We certainly wouldn't be bringing these creatures to writing workshops.

But how in the world can a workshop enhance, beef up, your individuality? I can no more make you an individual than you can make me statuesque.

Nor can any workshop discussion help you determine the individuality of your feelings amid all the sources, authentic and inauthentic, that feed them. The individuality of your emotions and the degree to which you feel these emotions may be crucial to the infectiousness of your art, but they are beyond the reach of instruction. You either experience the feelings you seek to convey deeply and honestly, or you do not. They are either real, or they are counterfeit. They either arise out of an emotion that defines the state of your soul, or they arise out of something else—your admiration for another writer's emotions; for an emotion you've seen dramatized on TV; for an emotion you would like to convince yourself, or someone else, you feel deeply; for the emotions (resentment, outrage, disdain, ennui) that everyone is currently talking about.

The feelings you wish to convey may be no more than an idea you came up with while outlining your novel.

But this is not to say, by the way, that the individuality of the feelings you express in your art is dependent on experience itself—that other bane of writing workshop conversation, "But it really happened."

Tolstoy puts it this way:

A boy, having experienced, let us say, fear on encountering a wolf, relates that encounter; and, in order to evoke in others the feeling he has experienced, describes himself, his condition before the encounter, the surroundings, the woods, his own lightheartedness, and then the wolf's appearance, its movements, the distance between himself and the wolf, etc. All this, if only the boy when telling the story again experiences the feelings he had lived through and infects the hearers and compels them to feel what the narrator has experienced, is art. If even the boy had not seen a wolf but had frequently been afraid of one, and if, wishing to evoke in others the fear he had felt, he invented an encounter with a wolf and recounted it so as to make his hearers share the feelings he experienced when he feared the wolf, that also would be art.

The individuality of the emotion you convey may have as its source a real encounter with a wolf or an imagined one, but the fact remains that the degree to which it is your emotion, deeply felt, cannot be adjusted or enhanced or changed in the least by advice, marginal notes, edits, or workshop consensus.

The same thing goes for sincerity. Tolstoy counts sincerity—that the artist be compelled by an inner need to express his feeling—as the most important of the three criteria for infectiousness. He says that when a reader sees that the artist is infected by his own writing and writes for himself, for no other reason than that he must, then the reader becomes infected, as well.

> Contrariwise, as soon as the spectator, hearer, or reader feels that the author is not writing, singing, or playing for his own satisfaction, does not himself feel what he wishes to express, but is doing it for him, the receiver, the reader, a resistance immediately springs up . . . and not only [does the work] fail to produce any infection but actually repels.

If you're worried about the declining sales of literary fiction, you might well attribute it to the fact that the reading public has developed just such a resistance. That overexposure to the pointed, posed, propagandized, insincere novels with a lesson to teach, an agenda to impose, has diminished our ability to be infected by true art—has, in fact, left some of us repelled by it. I've visited a fair number of book clubs, many of which seem to be made up of readers who just love everything they read (with the highest praise going to the "quick reads") or readers who are continually dissatisfied. Among the latter, the complaint I hear most often is some version of "I felt manipulated."

But who can teach you to be sincere? Isn't learned sincerity an oxymoron? Can sincerity be enhanced, deepened, embellished by instruction? Surely, sincerity as a means to an end is no longer sincerity. (Isn't there a joke about actors: if you can fake sincerity, you've got it made?) You may be compelled by an inner need to express your feelings when you write fiction, or you may be compelled by the vision of a chat with Oprah, revenge on an old lover, enhancements to your Facebook profile, or the envy of your workshop friends. Instruction cannot help you here. You are either sincerely attempting to infect your reader with what you have felt deeply, or you are doing something else.

Which leaves only clarity. Tolstoy has little to say about clarity. "The clearness of expression assists infection because the receiver who mingles in consciousness with the author is the better satisfied the more clearly the feeling is transmitted, which, as it seems to him, he had long known and felt, and for which he has only now found expression."

I like to imagine that Tolstoy says so little about clarity because he recognizes that here, at last, is something about the making of art that can indeed be taught in schools.

For while individuality and sincerity, or the lack thereof, can only be determined by a close examination of the writer's soul—something I am certain no workshop leader has the right or the inclination to do—clarity, clearness of expression, can be determined by a close examination of what is on the page.

It's been my experience that most writing workshops go awry when discussions of clarity, of the words on the page, give way to discussions of the author's, or of the characters', sincerity and individuality, when words like *motivation*, *psychology*, *symbol*, *theme*, *message*, *it really happened*, replace the simple question—a question, significantly enough, asked by generations of parents of small children in theaters, at sporting events, circuses, and parades—"Can you see?"

Reconsider for a moment Tolstoy's wolf-fearing boy. Even in this hypothetical—a boy who wants to infect his listeners with his own fear of encountering a wolf—Tolstoy the novelist understands that the boy cannot simply explain his fear but must describe "himself, his condition before the encounter, the surroundings, the woods, his own lightheartedness, and then the wolf's appearance, its movements, the distance between himself and the wolf." Tolstoy understands that in attempting to infect his listeners with his emotion, the boy must, first and foremost, become a little Joseph Conrad and "make them see." The woods, the wolf's movements, the distance between himself and the wolf. Clarity.

Here is Tolstoy himself in the opening page of his short masterpiece *Hadji Murad*:

> . . . he took hold of one of the cartridge pouches of his Circassian coat, but immediately let his hand drop and became silent on seeing two women enter the saklya.
>
> One was Sado's wife—the thin middle-aged woman who had arranged the cushions for Hadji Murad. The other was quite a young girl, wearing red trousers and a green beshmet. A necklace of silver coins covered the whole front of her dress, and at the end of the not long but thick plait of hard black hair that hung between her thin shoulder-blades a silver ruble was suspended. Her eyes, as sloe-black as those of her father and her brother, sparkled brightly in her young face, which tried to be stern. She did not look at the visitors, but evidently felt their presence.
>
> Sado's wife brought in a low round table, on which stood tea, pancakes in butter, cheese, churek (that is, thinly rolled out bread), and honey. The girl carried a basin, a ewer, and a towel.

Sado and Hadji Murad kept silent as long as the women, with their coin ornaments tinkling, moved softly about in their red soft-soled slippers, setting out before the visitors the things they had brought. Eldar sat motionless as a statue, his ram-like eyes fixed on his crossed legs, all the time the women were in the saklya. Only after they had gone, and their soft footsteps could no longer be heard behind the door, did he give a sigh of relief.

Can you see?

Clarity is achieved by careful use of detail—detail of place, detail of face, of dress and sound and smell and gesture. It is achieved by taking our time to get the sentence right, by eliminating the distractions of useless words and superfluous clauses, by having the courage to aim straight at our meaning rather than dance around it or bury it in pretentious obscurities. By taking our time, sentence by sentence, to develop a scene. By taking our time, sentence by sentence, to evoke a world and the creatures who inhabit it.

It is through clarity of expression that we become infected by the author's felt emotions, by his unique, sincere, might-as-well-be-my-own experience.

Ivan Ilyich knows firmly and indubitably that this is all nonsense and empty deception, but when the doctor, getting on his knees, stretched out, putting his ear now higher, now lower, and with a most significant face performs various gymnastic evolutions over him, Ivan Ilyich succumbs to it, as he used to succumb to lawyers' speeches, when he knew very well they were all lies and why they were lies.

The doctor, kneeling on the sofa, was still doing his tapping when the silk dress of Praskovya Fyodorovna rustled in the doorway and she was heard reproaching Pyotr for not announcing the doctor's arrival to her.

She comes in, kisses her husband, and at once begins to
insist that she was up long ago and it was only by misunderstanding that she was not there when the doctor came.

Ivan Ilyich looks at her, examines her all over, and reproaches
her for her whiteness, and plumpness, and the cleanness of her
hands, her neck, the glossiness of her hair, and the sparkle of her
eyes, so full of life. He hates her with all the forces of his soul.
And her touch makes him suffer from a flood of hatred for her.

—LEO TOLSTOY, *THE DEATH OF IVAN ILYICH*

Without the visual clarity, the physical authenticity of the scene—
the doctor putting his ear now higher, now lower, the rustle of the
silk dress in the doorway—that flood of emotion, of hatred, the
sincerity of it, the individuality of it, would never overtake us.

As parents of small children at movies and sporting events
and parades are well aware, we cannot feel (the thrill, the tension, the awe) if we cannot see.

John Barth has said that those of us who "teach" writing workshops are not teachers at all; we are coaches. I agree, and I like to
imagine us as we run along the sidelines—the margins, if you
will—of an apprentice work, shouting encouragement—"Keep
going!"—or warning—"Where are you going?"—but most of all
reminding the members of our team of this one, all-encompassing
question: "Is it clear? Are you being clear? Can we see?"

And here's the aspect of teaching art, of coaching art, that dear
Leo seems to miss: the result of that single injunction, that persistent mantra, can be (not always but often) the very thing that
inspires an apprentice writer to refine the language of a work-in-

progress to such an extent that it also becomes more sincere, more individual, more the writer's own.

Ask any group of literate English speakers to write a quick description of a certain person, place, or thing, and you will collect a group of similar nouns and adjectives, usually littered with the standard clichés. But then ask your writers to do it again, more precisely. And again, with more concentration and a completely different vocabulary. And then again, with another new set of words. Now each description begins to differentiate itself from all the others. Now each individual writer begins to focus on certain elements of the scene, the character, the object. Now each one—or most of them—notices something the others haven't. Now another draft, and not only has the individuality of each writer begun to display itself through the written word, the sincerity of the writer's pursuit also starts to become clear. Some of the group will fall away—"That's all I have to say about that"—and sometimes (perhaps due to a sincerity deficit; it happens) the entire group will fall away, exhausted, or content with that initial glance—"I liked it"—content with those comfortable clichés.

But if there is a writer in the group, an artist, each subsequent description will contain something new, and that something new will inspire the writer to look more closely, to see more clearly, to think about what's being described, what it means that this particular description has evolved in this particular way. Feelings will be evoked, perhaps even Tolstoy's "true impressions." Themes may even develop, themes about which the writer now has indeed thought. Sincerity is enhanced as mere assignment becomes revelation.

"Infection," Tolstoy writes, "is only obtained when an artist finds those infinitely minute degrees of which a work of art consists."

By teaching, *coaching*, clarity—"Can you see?"—those min-ute degrees may well be discovered. Infection may well ensue.

And so, to make peace with our Russian uncle, allow me to propose, then, that "Can you see?" is the only legitimate ques-tion a writing workshop should seek to answer.

But if it is asked with the same concern of that parent of a small child at a movie or a game or a parade, and if the remedy is sought with the same kindly parental determination (How about now? How about now?) when the answer is no, then coun-terfeit art can be avoided. Even in schools of art. Or in Florence, as the case may be.

FAITH AND LITERATURE

Every time I am asked to speak about faith, I grow more wary of the task. "Glibness," Flannery O'Connor wrote, "is the great danger in answering people's questions about religion."

I am sometimes called a Catholic writer—if for no more complex or compelling reason than the fact that most of my characters are Catholics (a symptom, perhaps, of the reading public's propensity to confuse the subject of a novel with its meaning)—and so I am often asked to answer questions about religion, about the role of faith, in my own work and sometimes even in the larger world.

My answers, even to my own ears, have become glib.

I write about Catholics first and foremost, I think, because the language of the Catholic Church provides my often reticent characters with a language for the things they would otherwise be unable to express: hopes, dreams, yearnings, fears. *Hail, Holy Queen, Mother of mercy, our life, our sweetness and our hope* or *Pray for us sinners, now and at the hour of our death* or *Never was it known that anyone who fled to your protection, implored your help, or sought your intercession was left unaided* or *Fill the hearts of your faithful, and enkindle in them the fire of your love* are all prayers that spring readily to mind for Catholics of a certain age, and yet these same Catholic men and women, my characters, would never say such lovely words out loud—*mercy, intercession, heart, enkindle, fire, love*—not in any sentence of their own design.

The Catholic Church gives my characters words for what they feel but cannot speak, much as a poet might do for the general population.

I write about Catholics because the promises of Christianity speak to the longing my characters feel as they make their way through their lives, the simple and consistent longing to make sense of suffering, of loss, of love, of their own unshakable feelings of exile and hope.

I write about Catholics because I am one, a cradle Catholic, and so I know the language and the detail. This saves me from having to do too much research. There's nothing more rewarding than spending hours and hours on the internet, picking up all kinds of historical or cultural tidbits, and nothing more deadening to one's prose than the determination to insert these interesting tidbits into a story, whether the story needs them or not. I write about a culture I know fairly well in order to resist the siren song of research—the procrastinating writer's best excuse for avoiding the far more difficult working at words.

Because I am a Catholic, I find that the notion of the sacramental—of the ordinary transformed into the extraordinary, of outward signs of inner grace—appeals to me and so finds its way into my work.

Because I am a Catholic, the language of ritual, its repetitions and refrains, appeals to me and so finds its way into my work.

The poet Thomas Lynch says that all writers are readers who "go karaoke"—a habit of reading begets a habit of writing—and

I suppose I could also say, without too much autobiographical self-analysis, that the habits of mind I formed as a cradle Catholic made me into one of those readers who dares to try her own hand.

Having been raised a Catholic, and having gone through the requisite turning away from religion in young adulthood—such a familiar and predictable loss of faith, so firmly associated in my mind with adolescent rebellion that even now I hear the whine of an indignant teenager in the voices of my peers who define themselves as "recovering Catholics"—I discovered in my apostate years that all the questions my faith had taught me to raise, all the questions my religion had attempted to answer, were currently under consideration in the world's great literature.

Not answered, mind you, but under long and serious and eloquent consideration.

I am a Catholic writer because my faith taught me to seek those answers, to reflect on our mortality, to rail against our suffering, to consider the grace by which we endure and the love that proposes to redeem us, and this habit of mind made me a reader of poetry and fiction and then, eventually, compelled me—a bit of karaoke—to try my own hand.

Yes, the glib reply to the religion question is that yes, my faith does indeed inform my fiction—of course it does—just as all experience informs what we write.

I sometimes tell young writers when they struggle with (mostly against) the autobiographical content of their writing that it is utterly impossible to leave your own experience out of your work. Language itself is acquired through experience. No parent (that I know of) has ever simply thrown a grammar book and a couple of language tapes into a baby's crib and returned once the child was fully versed. We all acquire our first language in a singular way, in a setting and a context that is unique for each individual, and so the very way we use language—our vocabulary, our metaphors, the cadence of our sentences, the way we shape our tales—arises out of our individual experience, and so all writing, especially creative writing, where the individuality of our voices is given free rein, is to some extent autobiographical.

So it is easy enough to count the ways being Catholic has informed my fiction. But what is perhaps not so evident, or so easy to explain, is how these many decades of working at words has informed my faith.

The American Catholic Church I was born into was an immigrant church—heavy on unquestioned rules and stately devotions and hushed mysteries, on listening to the Gospels at Mass but not so much on reading the Bible at home. (Another Catholic writer, Erin McGraw, once told me that her mother used to warn against reading the Bible too thoroughly, saying, "It will ruin your faith.")

I was raised in a Catholic Church that morphed just as I came of age into the more secular, less mystical, post–Vatican II Church in which Latin was jettisoned, the vernacular was spoken, and the old lofty rituals and formalities were transformed into something more ordinary, something that aligned itself more familiarly with the everyday.

In my adult life as a Catholic mother raising children in the Church, I've seen the fruits of that transformation in a younger generation that wastes no time on trivialities of religious style or outdated dogma, a generation of young Catholics—"practicing" or not—who embrace social justice as an integral part of their lives and their faith.

As an adult Catholic, I have also endured the pain and the anger, the disappointment, the humiliation, of the clergy abuse scandal and all the attendant, careening, moral failures of the hierarchy that this scandal has exposed. And I continue to be infuriated by the moral failure of the Church to admit women into the priesthood. I have grown fiercely impatient with the CEO-speak of the male Catholic hierarchy, cardinals and bishops and pastors alike, who have failed to see the Church's abuse crisis, the Church's entrenched misogyny, for what they are: existential challenges to the life, the very continuation, of the institution.

A rocky ride, then, this—a difficult, often maddening, journey, this lifelong adherence to the faith given to me at my birth. It is a journey that a good many of my "recovering Catholic" peers have refused to make and that I, too, might have abandoned long ago were it not for what my life as a fiction writer has taught me about faith.

Once, at a gathering of Irish poets in New York, I became involved in a conversation with an Irishwoman who had recently attended a lecture about the preponderance of undiagnosed schizophrenia in the Irish population. We shook our heads over this finding, wondering how much of it had to do with Catholicism, clergy abuse, health care, the Irish penchant for poetry, for secrets, or for drink. And then, at a pause in our solemn discussion, the woman said, only slightly tongue-in-cheek, "But honestly, don't you prefer a little madness—I mean, how dull it would be if we were all perfectly sane?"

I do not make light of the pain and the suffering, the confusion, the unalterable damage, my Church has inflicted; nor do I excuse its failings, its own fears and instances of moral blindness. But I know, too, that if it were otherwise, if the Catholic Church hummed along in utter perfection—consistent, sensible, fair, generous, no vanity, no pride, no instances of deceit or fear or any indication whatsoever of the foibles, yes, even the crimes, that we identify as human—I wouldn't want any part of it. The Kingdom of Heaven would have arrived on earth. Sinful, complex, maddening—and mad—human nature would have been usurped, or corrected, by the hand of the Divine, and there would be nothing more to see here . . . nothing left for the fiction writers to do, perhaps, than to sing the praises of this perfection. Pretty dull.

Those of us in the narrative arts need struggle and strife, the whole gamut of human failings and aspirations, all vice as well as all virtue. Disbelief as well as belief. As O'Connor points out in the same letter in which she talks about glibness, the Church was founded on Peter, who denied Christ three times and could not walk on water. Why are we expecting perfection from his successors?

Or, I might add, from ourselves?

Many of the characters I am most drawn to in my reading, and in my writing life, are full of questions, not answers. Many are terrible people. With Flannery O'Connor in mind, I think of Mrs. Turpin in the short story "Revelation." Mrs. Turpin is a devout farm wife who finds herself attacked in the waiting room of her doctor's office by a demented young woman who calls her "a wart hog from hell." Later that day, while watering her own hogs, Mrs. Turpin confronts God:

> "What do you send me a message like that for?" she said in a low fierce voice, barely above a whisper but with the force of a shout in its concentrated fury. "How am I a hog and me both? How am I saved and from hell too?"
>
> . . . "Why me?" she rumbled. "It's no trash around here, black or white, that I haven't given to. And break my back to the bone every day working. And do for the church."
>
> . . . In the deepening light everything was taking on a mysterious hue. The pasture was growing a peculiar glassy green and the streak of highway had turned lavender. She

braced herself for a final assault and this time her voice rolled out over the pasture. "Go on," she yelled, "call me a hog! Call me a hog again. From hell. Call me a wart hog from hell. Put that bottom rail on top. There'll still be top and bottom!"

A garbled echo returned to her.

A final surge of fury shook her and she roared, "Who do you think you are?"

Or this, from the character of Lily Briscoe, a middle-aged painter in Virginia Woolf's *To the Lighthouse*. Dear and delightful Mrs. Ramsay has died, and Lily is once again painting a landscape on the lawn of the summer house where Mrs. Ramsay was once the hostess. Beside her is Augustus Carmichael, a poet.

For one moment she felt that if they both got up, here, now, on the lawn, and demanded an explanation, why was it so short, why was it so inexplicable, said it with violence, as two fully equipped human beings from whom nothing should be hid might speak, then, beauty would roll itself up; the space would fill; the empty flourishes would form into shape; if they shouted loud enough Mrs. Ramsay would return.

Human, sinful, loving, mortal, outraged, shouting or pleading, the characters I am drawn to in fiction are full of questions, many of them furious—questions but not, necessarily, answers. They are not, in other words, glib.

Some years ago there was a short-lived commotion (Is there anything in our public discourse these days that's not short-lived?) among the professional atheists and the professional defenders of the faith regarding the release of some of Mother Teresa's personal letters in a book called *Mother Teresa: Come Be My Light*. Letters that described, quite painfully, her years of lost faith.

"When I try to raise my thoughts to heaven," she wrote to her confessor, "there is such convicting emptiness that those very thoughts return like sharp knives and hurt my very soul . . ."

And in another letter: "The silence and emptiness is so great that I look and do not see, listen and do not hear."

As you might recall, her defenders concluded that the excruciating doubt with which she lived for decades, even as she accomplished her work, was further proof of her saintliness. Her detractors claimed that her doubt only revealed the hypocrisy of her public life, only illustrated the unsustainable self-delusion that is religious faith.

(The fact that the letters, which she'd written on the advice of her confessor and had asked to have destroyed upon her death, were published at all might have led to what is, to my mind, a far more interesting discussion about the value we, believers and nonbelievers alike, place on any inner life, or spiritual life, any emotional experience—call it what you will—that is not made public, revealed in a memoir, or "shared" in a TV interview. About what value we place on what is, and remains, personal and private—kept silently by one individual soul, or between one individual soul and her God. A more interesting discussion might ensue were we to ask if we even believe that the inner life, the unexpressed [untweeted?] thought or emotion, has any value at all. Do we believe the inner life, unexpressed, even exists?)

When the letters were published, I was asked—as a "public" Catholic—to offer an opinion on the debate in a talk for a local Christian group. I was up to my elbows in another novel, and so my initial, somewhat distracted reaction to the whole debate was, I'm afraid, glib: Doubt, well, yes, of course, she was plagued by doubt. There's always doubt.

My initial reaction was to recall the mantra of the aging writer in Henry James's short story "The Middle Years": "We work in the dark—we do what we can—we give what we have. Our doubt is our passion, and our passion is our task. All the rest is the madness of art."

Given the passion revealed in Mother Teresa's heartfelt letters to her confessors—"Those very thoughts return like sharp knives and hurt my very soul"—it occurred to me that it would not be out of line to propose that the pain she felt was equivalent to that of James's character: *We work in the dark. We do what we can. We give what we have. Our doubt is our passion. Our passion is our task. All the rest is the madness of faith.*

My initial reaction, then, without thinking much about it, was to conflate the two: art and religious belief. The creative process and the process of faith.

I say process of faith, not achievement of faith, not even leap (with a hard or soft landing) of faith, but process, an edging forward and a falling back, a holding of one's breath, a letting go, a groping in the dark, working in the dark toward something— some perfection—we yearn for, strive for. Faith as work, just as art is work. Faith and art both as processes that do not continually guarantee progress: you write a sentence, then you cross it out, and then you write it again. You make progress in your novel, and then you don't. You raise your questioning voice in prayer, and there is comfort. You try it again, and there is none.

The process of faith and the creative process: both a struggle to apprehend something, some perfection, that we suspect from the outset is unattainable but that we seek nevertheless to achieve.

In his poem "The Excursion," Wordsworth writes of

> One in whom persuasion and belief
> Had ripened into faith, and faith become
> A passionate intuition.

In both the creative process and the process of faith, we feel that passionate intuition.

My experience as a writer, my long association with writers young and old, assures me that this much is true: we all begin in doubt (although the extent to which we admit this varies greatly). We begin in uncertainty: Are we up to the task? Are we smart enough? Talented enough? Is our material sufficient? Is our vision clear? Are we crazy to do this?

We suspect that the answer is no to all the former—a resounding yes to the last. (In fact, the simple question, Am I crazy to be doing this, writing this novel?—and its corollary: My parents think I'm crazy to be doing this—is a major topic of conversation in my individual conferences with MFA students.)

But we are also passionate in our doubt, as passionate to confirm our fears as we are to allay them.

I'm not sure any of us involved in this mad pursuit can say why. *Driven* is the word that most often comes to mind. Driven to try. Perhaps it is because the world as it is, as we find it, is incomplete, inaccessible, unacceptable without the filter of art. Perhaps because the unexamined life is not worth living, and writing fiction is our way of examining life. Perhaps because a story or a character or language itself compels us. Because we are compelled. Because we must.

And so, with no guarantee of the outcome but with a passionate intuition, we begin the pursuit, the story, the novel, the poem. We write a sentence and cross it out.

In my years of teaching novice fiction writers, I have rarely—never, I would venture to say—seen a first draft of a story that did not contain something, perhaps a detail, a gesture, a phrase, a metaphor or motif, that the writer had not anticipated before the work was begun and, often enough, had not even noticed until after I pointed it out. More often than not these unanticipated bits of narrative are among the most interesting things in an early draft, an indication of some complexity of style or complication of plot or felicity of language that the writer, starting out, didn't know the story would contain and yet recognizes immediately as essential to all that will follow.

It's one of my favorite moments in a conference: when a student writer looks at his or her own work with a kind of awe, saying, "I just threw that in there"—that detail, that phrase, that motif—"but now I see how it belongs."

This is the creative process.

Every novel and story—I daresay, every work of art—begins with a vague ideal. I say ideal, not idea, as in, Where do you get your ideas? An idea for a novel or story—that is, what the story will be about, what will happen in its plot, what characters it will contain—is easy enough to come by. You can't be introduced as a novelist to a group of strangers at a cocktail party without hearing at least one great idea for a novel before the night is through.

But the ideal for a story is something else altogether. It is the barely understood, barely apprehended notion of a novel's perfect rhythm and shape, its goal, its meaning. The ideal for a work is, somehow, the beating heart of whatever it is that compels us to write, but it is also, at the outset, vague, unformed, clouded by doubt. It only really begins to reveal itself, slowly, perhaps subconsciously, through the difficult work of writing each sentence, choosing each word, constructing each scene, and in the course of this hard work, if we are fortunate, we stumble upon the unanticipated detail, the motif, the character that changes everything.

When these small, unexpected, serendipitous revelations occur—and they hardly occur daily, or even regularly, and much work must be done, many sentences written and crossed out, to achieve them—the doubt that we all begin with fades, and the artist, the writer, begins to see his or her own work more clearly. The vague ideal for the work—its perfect form—barely apprehended at the outset, now appears to be striving to reveal itself, to make itself known through the choices the writer has made, choices whose significance to the work as a whole surprises even the author.

"Art happens," Margaret Atwood wrote. "It happens when you have the craft and the vocation and are waiting for something else, something extra, or maybe not waiting; in any case, it happens. It's the extra rabbit coming out of the hat, the one you didn't put there."

These delightful and unexpected choices, these rabbits you didn't put there, may be guided by any number of things: talent, we might say. The subconscious, yes. By good luck, by serendipity. We might simply call them inspired. But it is through these happy choices that the story (and the poem, the painting, the sculpture, the music) makes itself known to the artist and, through the artist, makes itself known to the world.

As I thought about Mother Teresa's letters, it became clear to me that the process of faith is much the same. We begin in doubt—doubt in ourselves, in our capacity to believe, in our ability to remain steady in our belief. We doubt the forms of religious faith—the doctrine, the ritual, the language itself—doubt especially the great promises of a religion like Christianity: forgiveness, peace, eternal life, love that redeems us. Promises that can so often sound to the contemporary mind like so much wishful thinking.

But even amid this doubt there remains the longing for sense, for justice, for our experience of life—our joy, our pain, what we know of love and awe and despair—to find a greater context than the narrow limits of our years alive. We strive, we are driven, as the creative artist is driven, to remake the world as we find it into something more reasonable, more sensible, more just. We apprehend, we intuit, vaguely, vaguely, the form of that perfection, and we are driven to pursue it, knowing, suspecting, fearing all the while that we are not up to the task, that it will remain, finally, unattainable, unbelievable, but we pursue it nevertheless.

And sometimes in that pursuit of faith, as in the pursuit of art, through our daily work at it, our groping in the dark, we stumble upon moments of insight, inspiration—moments of grace, if you will—that, for an instant, allay doubt. Perhaps for the saintly among us—the religious pilgrims, the faith-seeking scientist or naturalist, the close personal friends of the Holy Spirit—these moments occur frequently, maybe even with a bit of drama—a *eureka*, a sharp intake of breath, a vision, a transcendent high five.

But having observed the creative process—mine and others'—over the years, I have more experience with those moments that seem to occur inadvertently, those moments that surprise us with their significance . . . just as those meaningful first-draft details surprise their young authors.

I am more familiar with those moments that occur not as a miraculous parting of the waters or even a marvelous changing of water into wine but as the unexpected, unanticipated confluence of ordinary circumstances from which—for just a moment—we not only glimpse the unattainable ideal but sense that this perfection seeks to make itself known to us.

In his Nobel Prize acceptance speech, Saul Bellow said:

The essence of our real condition, the complexity, the confusion, the pain of it is shown to us in glimpses, in what Proust and Tolstoy thought of as "true impressions." The essence reveals, and then conceals itself. When it goes away, it leaves us again in doubt. But we never seem to lose our connection with the depths from which these glimpses come. The sense of our real powers, the powers we seem to derive from the universe itself, also comes and goes. We are reluctant to talk about this because our language is inadequate and because few people are willing to risk talking about it. They would have to say, "There is a spirit," and that is taboo.

The essence reveals, and then conceals itself. When it goes away, it leaves us again in doubt.

I've said that the creative process—like the process of faith—begins in doubt.

But I have come to understand that the creative process is also, continually, sustained by doubt.

In my years of teaching and writing, I have discovered that there is no surer formula for the failure of a story or a novel than the author's certainty—from the beginning and throughout the process—that he or she *knows*, knows from the outset the story's beginning and end and every permutation of character and plot. The confident writer, the control-freak writer, the writer who cannot let go of his plan, is sure to be the writer whose work will remain pedestrian, predictable, uninspired.

(The fact that bookstores and the bestseller lists are crowded with such work is beside the point.)

Henry James:

A novel is in its broadest definition a personal, a direct impression of life; that, to begin with, constitutes its value, which is greater or less according to the intensity of the impression. But there will be no intensity at all, and therefore no value, unless there is freedom to feel and say. The tracing of a line to be followed, of a tone to be taken, of a form to be filled out, is a limitation of that freedom and a suppression of the very thing we are most curious about.

Flaubert put it more simply: "If I tried to insert action, I should be following a rule and would spoil everything."

Without doubt—in the creative process, as well as in the process of religious faith—we are often simply following along, filling out forms, limiting our freedom to be taken by surprise by those true impressions that constitute our unexpected moments of grace, those unexpected moments in which our Creator, or the ideal form of the novel, attempts to make itself known to us.

Complete certainty, total adherence to dogma, to foregone conclusions, to the glib reply, cuts us off—in art as well as in faith—from revelation, from the discovery of what we didn't know we knew. Smug assuredness, in faith and in the creative arts, cuts us off from those glimpses of essence, of perfection, of what seeks to reveal itself, that we didn't even know enough to look for but that strike us, if only momentarily, as exactly what we'd hoped to find.

Thornton Wilder wrote that "the response we make when we 'believe' a work of the imagination is that of saying: 'This is the way things are. I have always known it without being fully aware that I knew it.'"

The effort to come into full awareness of what we've always known—however brief that awareness might be—is the work of both faith and literature.

Allow me a very pedestrian (in more ways than one) illustration:

Not long after I was asked to devise a lecture that would address the commotion over Mother Teresa's letters, I was in my office at Johns Hopkins in Baltimore. I use this office only one day a week, and then only to meet with students, and so my bookshelves there have become a repository for the overflow of my colleagues, past and present. I usually drive the fifty miles between my home in Bethesda and Baltimore, but on this day my car was in the shop, and I took the train. It was early in the semester. I'd already read that week's stack of student papers, and I'd finished the book I was carrying on the ride up. Now I wanted something to read on the train going home. But since the trip was going to involve a bus, Amtrak, the D.C. Metro, as well as a stop at the grocery store, I didn't want anything, literally, heavy. So I scanned my shelves—which contained a good many thick anthologies—with the intention of finding a book that was physically small and light.

The smallest book on my shelf that day was a yellowing 1982 edition of C. S. Lewis's *Screwtape Letters*, a book given to a now retired professor at Hopkins by a freshman student—or so the note inside indicated—in 1990. I like C. S. Lewis well enough, although I've always agreed with Roald Dahl's Matilda that *The Chronicles of Narnia* sorely lacks "funny bits." While I'd never read the book, I knew the premise of *The Screwtape Letters*: letters of advice from a senior devil, Screwtape, to his nephew Wormwood, an apprentice demon. I always thought that the premise seemed somewhat dated, exaggerated, coy. But now, I thought (so to speak), what the hell. I slipped the book into my purse and began reading on the train.

And there, on page 36, I read about what Screwtape calls "the law of Undulation."

"Humans are amphibians," he tells Wormwood.

Half spirit, half animal . . . as spirits they belong to the eternal world, but as animals they inhabit time. This means that while their spirit can be directed to the eternal world, their bodies, passions, and imaginations are in continual change, for to be in time means to change. Their nearest approach to constancy, therefore, is undulation—the repeated return to a level from which they repeatedly fall back, a series of troughs and peaks.

"If you had watched your patient carefully," he goes on to say, "you would have seen this undulation in every department of his life—his interest in his work, his affection for his friends, his physical appetites, all go up and down. As long as he lives on earth, periods of emotional and bodily richness and liveliness will alternate with periods of numbness and poverty."

"The Enemy," Wormwood says (meaning God), "is prepared to do a little overriding at the beginning.

He will set them [meaning us] off with communications of His presence which, though faint, seem great to them, with emotional sweetness, and easy conquest over temptation. But God never allows this state of affairs to last long. Sooner or later, He withdraws, if not in fact, then at least from their conscious experience, all those supports and incentives. He leaves the creature to stand upon its own legs, to carry out from the will alone duties that have lost all relish . . .

We work in the dark—we do what we can. We give what we have. Our doubt is our passion.

The essence reveals, and then conceals itself. When it goes away, it leaves us again in doubt.

Or, Flaubert again: "Sometimes, when I am empty, when words don't come, when I find I haven't written a single sentence after scribbling whole pages, I collapse on my couch and lie there dazed, bogged down in a swamp of despair . . . A quarter of an hour later, everything has changed; my heart is pounding with joy." Undulation.

"Do not be deceived, Wormwood," Screwtape continues. "Our cause [the corruption of the soul] is never more in danger than when a human, no longer desiring but still intending to do God's will, looks around upon a universe from which every trace of Him seems to have vanished, and asks why he has been forsaken, and still obeys."

I am quite certain that if I had set out with the intention of finding a way to think about, to speak about, Mother Teresa's faith and doubt, I could not have found anything more pertinent than this. Had I done an internet search to find a theological companion piece to James's quote from *The Middle Years* or Bellow's from his Nobel speech, I could not have found anything more apt than Lewis's law of Undulation—which came into my hands not because I was looking for it, but because the car was in the shop and I'd finished my other reading and I didn't want to carry anything heavy and nearly two decades ago a student had given a professor a book that proved to be the smallest thing on my shelf.

Because I'd been asked to say something about Mother Teresa's loss of faith, and I doubted very much that I'd find anything at all to say that wasn't glib.

In the same letter in which Flannery O'Connor pointed out how easy glibness is, she also said: "The Holy Spirit very rarely shows Himself on the surface of anything . . . It is what is invisible that God sees and what the Christian must look for."

To which I can only add, "Writers, too." Catholic or otherwise.

Look, artistic inspiration, like religious faith, does not come to most of us with the beating of wings or the leaping of flames or the cinematic, middle-of-the-night *aha* moment that cuts to an acceptance speech in Stockholm. It comes through long effort, through moving ahead and falling back, through working in the dark. It comes to us in moments of passionate intuition and over long days and nights of painful silence. It arrives in the usual and yet miraculous confluence of ordinary events. It comes and goes. It leaves us in doubt. It is sustained by doubt. It is the work of a lifetime.

ALL DRAMA IS FAMILY DRAMA

It was Moss Hart, not Eugene O'Neill, who made me want to be a playwright when I was young. The theatrical eccentricities of the mad family in *You Can't Take It with You* bore little resemblance to my own doggedly genteel, determinedly reserved Irish American clan, but there was enough metaphorical affinity between the literal fireworks being assembled in the basement in the Hart/Kaufman play and the pyrotechnic potential of all that went unsaid at my own family gatherings to suggest to me, early on, that family life was best captured onstage. It should be madcap, comical: eccentric uncles in the basement, fey ballerina sisters twirling by, wild entrances, floorboard-pounding exits. It should be crazy, funny, wry. Oh, God, families.

What I knew of Eugene O'Neill I knew mostly from Groucho Marx's take on *Strange Interlude* in *Animal Crackers*—funny stuff.

And then, as a dutiful English major, I went to see *Long Day's Journey into Night*. Of course I recognized certain familial traits: the fragile gentility, the easy recriminations, the incendiary nature of the long unspoken when it is doused with alcohol. Yet the play also opened my eyes to what I had already resolved to resist. In the modern way, and with my own bias against too much high-toned emotion, I had resolved to resist taking for the subject of my fiction that overworked, overwrought drama that was family life.

And yet, O'Neill's play was an acknowledgment of the legitimacy of the drama of family life, of the terribleness of family love, the awful burden of parental, filial, fraternal love. But the play was also, in all its seriousness, its yearning, its grim poetry, a paean to the dignity of that terribleness.

O'Neill understood the depth of our longing to love those to whom we are "in tears and blood" forever bound. He understood the inevitability of our failure to do so. The awkwardness of this—the missteps and missed connections, the slammed doors and startling explosions—is the stuff of comedy. But the pain of it is written on the bone. O'Neill knew this. In *Long Day's Journey* he elevated that pain, made it finer, nobler, certainly more eloquent, than it ever appears to be in real, hapless, family life.

It was a transformation that struck me as a miracle of sorts, back then: all those familiar Irish American traits made heartbreaking and universal and new.

It strikes me the same way still.

VOICE-OVERS

More and more I am amazed, and sometimes dismayed, by how often apprentice writers recoil from the very notion of exposition. Young writers whose characters are without scruple, whose scenes of sex, violence, cruelty, and savagery are vividly described in excruciating detail, will sit back like indignant Fundamentalists when I mildly suggest that they simply tell the reader that their hero was raised by circus clowns in Siberia rather than develop a lengthy scene in which our hero goes to Starbucks and orders a frothy skim latte from a pretty barista who, when she takes her break and joins him at his table *ringed* with coffee stains, begins a conversation in which she mentions that she has tickets to the *Ringling* Brothers that night, to which he can reply, "Funny you should mention the circus, because my parents were actually Russian circus clowns . . . ," and thus deliver to the story, and to the eavesdropping reader, his background via dialogue and scene: showing, not telling.

"You mean," the outraged young writer says, "you want me to just *say* it?"

Yes, I more and more wearily reply. For God's sake, just say it. Tell us what we need to know, and get on with your story.

In his study of the short story called *The Lonely Voice*, Frank

O'Connor writes: "There are three necessary elements in a story—exposition, development, and drama. Exposition we may illustrate as 'John Fortescue was a solicitor in the little town of X'; development as 'One day Mrs. Fortescue told him she was about to leave him for another man'; and drama as 'You will do nothing of the kind,' he said."

Notice how even in O'Connor's three-line example, exposition and development work to inform drama: how what we've been told about the character enhances what we are shown. "You will do nothing of the kind," Mr. Fortescue says. Of course he would put it this way: he's a solicitor in the little town of X. We recognize his character, the sound of his voice, in those seven spoken words because first we've been told something about him and his current circumstances, something that informs and enhances our reading of the dialogue.

In just two sentences of exposition, character has begun to form, and as a result, we don't read the quoted dialogue to be informed of something we need to know, some bit of essential background ("Funny you should mention . . ."). We read the dialogue with a sense of our own sagacity—that is so him. And to find out what will happen to Mr. and Mrs. Fortescue next.

In short, exposition makes drama.

I've been known, in writing workshops, to use this example: We are an hour into class, and the door opens, and a small, middle-aged woman walks in. I nod to her, and she returns the nod and takes a chair in the back of the room. Another hour goes by. We begin to discuss a story, one that everybody's already read, about a tired mother losing her temper as she puts her young son to bed. At one point during the discussion, the woman in the back of the room lets out a long sigh.

Now, consider the same scenario, but this time, at the beginning of the workshop, I mention to the class that a friend of mine might be stopping by. She's asked to sit in on the class, I say, because she's attempting to write a memoir. She's just finished serving a thirty-year prison sentence for the murder of her five-year-old child. Now, an hour into class, when the door opens, members of the workshop will observe the woman in a new way. They will give meaning to the details of her appearance that the details alone don't possess—those 1980s-style shoulder pads in her jacket, for instance, or the way she shuffles her feet, the defeated way she nods. They'll anticipate, anxiously, the last story to be discussed, the one about the impatient mother. Suspense begins to build, and when, during the discussion of that story, she lets out a long sigh, it will have meaning.

There will be drama in the room, not merely incident, not merely "scene," all because of a few lines of exposition. Because of a few lines of exposition, some telling prior to showing, there will be not merely the sight of the character with her puzzling clothes and her shuffling gait, there will be a sense, as well, of what I like to call the *why* of her—why the clothes, why the shuffle, why the sigh.

Such telling, of course, especially to our twenty-first-century eyes and ears, takes a certain amount of hubris and a great deal of caution. An author must claim the authority to "tell" but also have the ability to stop "telling"—to get out of the way—as the scene begins.

Elsewhere in *The Lonely Voice*, O'Connor puts it this way:

> Drama is the proof that the writer offers of the truth of his narrative, and should be used only in this way. It should always have the electrifying effect it has in a Greek play when the voice of the Chorus stops and we see the specific illustration of what we have heard as poetic generalization. In storytelling the reader should be aware that the storyteller's voice has stopped.

I would add that the writer should be aware of this, as well.

It's a tricky business, and even the most adroit storytellers can trip on it a bit. Jhumpa Lahiri's gorgeous novel *The Namesake* opens with a close third-person point of view: "On a sticky August evening two weeks before her due date, Ashima Ganguli stands in the kitchen of a Central Square apartment combining Rice Krispies and Planters peanuts and chopped red onion in a bowl." The narrative quickly moves into Ashima's consciousness: "A curious warmth floods her abdomen . . ."

And continues in that limited third-person consciousness, "In the bathroom she discovers on her underpants a solid streak of brown blood. She calls out to her husband, Ashoke, a doctoral student in electrical engineering at MIT, who is studying in the bedroom."

That awkward bit of exposition—"a doctoral student in electrical engineering at MIT"—is surely not what poor Ashima is thinking about her husband at this intimate and dramatic moment. Somehow a narrator has followed her into the bathroom and now speaks to the reader from over her head—voiceover—in order to fill us in on Ashoke's résumé while Ashima herself is otherwise absorbed.

There is a parallel here to the screenwriter's trade. Even films that use voice-over well, that open beautifully with spoken narration ("Last night I dreamt I went to Manderley again"), do so with the unspoken promise that soon, and fairly soon, the narrator will get out of the way, fall silent, so that the moviegoer there in the dark can be absorbed into the scene, the screen, the character's point of view, the movie itself.

One of my first encounters with Hollywood occurred just after the publication of my second novel. My agent had a call from an up-and-coming young producer who wanted to know if I would be willing to fly to New York to meet with a Very

Famous Director who was interested in directing a film version of my book if I would write the screenplay.

I was intrigued but uncertain. I've never subscribed to the notion that a film adaptation is the final imprimatur for a work of fiction, despite how often I've been told by encouraging friends and strangers, "Maybe they'll make a movie of your novel," as if I'd been aiming for a screenplay all along but somehow missed the mark and wrote a novel by mistake.

Deep in my prose writer's heart, I also retain the notion that any novel's inability to translate well to film is not a failure of the written document, but proof of its superiority.

I'm also extremely wary of artistic collaborations of any sort. I'm not gregarious or assertive, and although I'm easily convinced of the brilliance of other people's ideas, I'm also given to disagreeing with those brilliant ideas on first hearing, just for the hell of it. I suspect that, like most of us who write novels, I want to be in charge of everything: story, direction, casting, wardrobe, lighting, dialogue, catering, and transportation.

I was living in San Diego at the time the young producer called. He was in L.A., and so was the director. I suppose it told me everything I needed to know about the difference between dealing with New York publishing types and dealing with Hollywood movie types that we all met for dinner in New York.

The experience was Hollywood all the way: a limo to take me to the airport, first-class tickets, a limo to take me to my hotel on Central Park South. An elaborate tea that afternoon with the producer, who was charming and boyish and enthusiastic in an Andy Hardy "Let's put on a show in the barn" kind of way about the prospects of this movie "happening." Later, at the appointed time, my agent and I went from my hotel to yet another limo, where the director was waiting. He was smoking a cigar. Of course he was. Wearing sunglasses. Of course. He took my fingertips in his and asked, in a heavy Eastern European accent, "Is this the hand that wrote that beautiful book?"

Then he sat back and said, "Here's what you need to know about making movies."

First, he said, get all your money up front. No movie ever makes a profit on paper.

Second, he said, when you write the screenplay for me, forget the novel. In your novel, he said, there's that wonderful narrator's voice. Beautiful. In the movie, forget it. Narrators never work. Voice-overs never work. Everyone tries it; it never works. Your screenplay, he said, should tell me, "Here's the door. Here's who comes through the door. Here's what he says." That's all. Forget narrators.

Of course, contrarian that I am, I thought immediately of movie adaptations that seemed to contradict this theory—*To Kill a Mockingbird* and *Sophie's Choice* came to mind—but I said nothing at all. I was, I admit, pretty starstruck there in the stretch limo, even as I felt myself bristle at his words "Forget the novel."

"A novel is not a movie," the Famous Director told me over dinner. (He ordered the bratwurst; of course he did.) "You know how to write a novel. I'll teach you how to write a movie." And then he repeated his mantra: Here is the door. Here is who comes through the door. Here is what he says. Scene. Dialogue. Movement. Nobody talking at me out of nowhere, he said. No voice-overs.

Since this advice was given to me in my younger and more vulnerable years, I've been turning it over in my mind ever since, and so, appropriately enough, it returned to me again when I watched yet another adaptation of *The Great Gatsby*—one of those novels, I would contend, whose failure to translate successfully to the screen indicates its superiority as a book, only a book.

The Great Gatsby has been made into a movie four times, with varying results. The latest two attempts, from 1974 and 2013, both make liberal use of voice-over. In fact, in the 2013 version, Nick Carraway not only narrates via voice-over but also writes—literally writes, at the urging of his psychiatrist—*The Great Gatsby* while in a sanatorium, recovering from alcohol addiction and a nervous breakdown.

It struck me when I saw the film that there were many things wrong with this premise. First, it forced the audience to endure a number of scenes in which Nick is seen writing—certainly one of the most unintentionally hilarious clichés of moviemaking, for how do you make dramatic, or even interesting, a character typing (or, as the case may be, scribbling), not typing, staring into space, then typing again?

(I saw the movie version of *The Hours* with my book club, a very sincere and generous group of avid readers, and even they began to chuckle when Nicole Kidman as Virginia Woolf indicated to the audience that she was thinking about her writing by silently and unhappily moving her pursed lips, as if *Mrs. Dalloway* was a broken molar in the back of her mouth or a remnant of sour candy melting on her tongue.)

Second, it reinforced the notion of writing as therapy. I have nothing against writing as therapy; I'm happy to champion it. But writing as therapy is a very different experience from the careful, painstaking, fully intentional composition of sentence after sentence that is the pursuit of the literary artist, that was, in fact, Fitzgerald's own difficult, disciplined, fully intentional pursuit of his art. (His short autobiography begins like this: "The history of my life is the history of the struggle between an overwhelming urge to write and a combination of circumstances bent on keeping me from it.")

Third, this setup leads to the film ending with a closing shot of the finished manuscript and a title page that reads *The Great Gatsby by Nick Carraway*, which I feared would screw up an entire generation's AP American lit test scores.

But mostly what this premise distorts is the motivation—the overwhelming urge—of the literary artist to write. It seems to admit that unless prompted, confined, assigned, no sane person, no sane narrator, is going to just start whispering a story into an unknown reader's ear. Just as no moviegoer will endure for long some voice "out of nowhere" talking into the theater.

Granted, this writing-from-the-sanatorium premise might have been a legitimate attempt to mitigate that sense of "out of nowhere," of the storyteller's voice suddenly speaking, unprompted, into the dark—the kind of voice-over Horton Foote (for instance) chose for his screenplay for *To Kill a Mockingbird*, since that movie, after all, doesn't begin with a grown-up Scout, dressed in black because she has just returned from Atticus's funeral, sitting at her typewriter in her Atlanta law office, with Truman Capote somewhere in the room saying, "Why don't you write about that summer Boo Radley saved your life?"

But while I watched this particular *Gatsby*, it occurred to me that in every case the movie voice-over remains a way for the filmmaker to duplicate—ham-handedly, the Famous Director would argue—the experience of reading, not watching, a story. And it fails, he was perhaps suggesting, because there really is no duplicating the experience of reading a novel.

There is no truly equivalent experience in life to "hearing" the voice of another human being who is "speaking" to us from the silence of the page. The intimacy of the experience of reading cannot be duplicated satisfactorily by film because a movie must, in one way or another, speak out loud. It must show, not tell: here is the door, here's who comes through it, this is what he says. Film must make do with sight and sound, while the novelist has sight and sound and taste and touch and smell, because the novelist has voice and, through voice, the great good tool of exposition.

Because until books come with vials of scent or *Pat the Bunny* swatches of material or some version of Bertie Bott's Every Flavour Beans for readers to slip into their mouths when they encounter certain pages, these handy senses will not appear unless the writer *tells* the reader about them.

And yet, I suspect it is because of these cinematic models—because our sense of "scene" has been so shaped by "screen"—that more and more I find prose writers who limit themselves to the screenwriter's tools alone—sight and sound—while taste, touch, and smell, which demand exposition, go unmentioned and unexplored.

But consider this sweet poem by Nickole Brown:

FOR MY GRANDMOTHER'S PERFUME, NORELL

Because your generation didn't wear perfume
    but chose a scent—a signature—every day
        you spritzed a powerhouse floral with top
            notes of lavender and mandarin, a loud
smell one part Doris Day, that girl-next-door
    who used Technicolor to find a way to laugh about
        husbands screwing their secretaries over lunch,
            the rest all Faye Dunaway, all high drama
extensions of nails and lashes, your hair a
    a breezy fall of bangs, a stiletto entrance
        that knew to walk sideways, hip first:
            now watch a *real* lady descend the stairs.

Launched in 1968, Norell
    was the 1950s tingling with the beginning

of Disco; Norell was a housewife tired of gospel,
        mopping her house to Stevie Wonder instead.

You wore so much of it, tiny pockets
    of your ghost lingered hours after you
        were gone, and last month, I stalked
            a woman wearing your scent through
the grocery so long I abandoned
    my cart and went home. Fanny, tell me:
        How can manufactured particles carry you
            through the air? I always express what I see,
but it was no photo that
    stopped and queased me to my knees.

After all these years, you were an invisible
    trace, and in front of a tower of soup cans
        I was a simple animal craving the deep memory
            worn by a stranger oblivious of me. If I had courage,
the kind of fool I'd like to be,
    I would have pressed my face to her small
        shoulder, and with the sheer work of
            two pink lungs, I would have breathed
enough to
    conjure
        you back
            to me.

I know I don't have to make a big case for how evocative the
sense of smell is in our lives, and yet I am continually surprised
by how neglected the handiest of the five senses is in my students' writing. I've actually taken to looking at the beginnings

of stories and novels just to see how many pages go by before a smell is mentioned—try it.

So here are the first sentences of Chimamanda Ngozi Adichie's novel *Americanah*:

> Princeton, in the summer, smelled of nothing, and although Ifemelu liked the tranquil greenness of the many trees, the clean streets and stately homes . . . it was this, the lack of a smell, that most appealed to her, perhaps because the other American cities she knew well had all smelled distinctly. Philadelphia had the musty scent of history. New Haven smelled of neglect. Baltimore smelled of brine, and Brooklyn of sunwarmed garbage.

You can't film that.

Or from chapter 2 of Sandra Cisneros's *The House on Mango Street*:

> But my mother's hair, my mother's hair, like little rosettes, like little candy circles all curly and pretty because she pinned it in pincurls all day, sweet to put your nose into when she is holding you, holding you and you feel safe, is the warm smell of bread before you bake it, is the smell when she makes room for you on her side of the bed still warm with her skin, and you sleep near her, the rain outside falling and Papa snoring. The snoring, the rain, and Mama's hair that smells like bread.

Taste, of course, needs no other champion than Proust and his madeleine, although I love Lorrie Moore's description of whiskey truffles in *Who Will Run the Frog Hospital?*: "One feels the captured storm in these, a warm storm under the tongue." But just to belabor my point a bit, consider the madeleine scene, which is probably referenced these days far more than it's read and is, of course, pure exposition:

> . . . one day in winter, as I returned home, my mother, seeing that I was cold, suggested that, contrary to my habit, I have a little tea. I refused at first and then, I do not know why, changed my mind. She sent for one of those squat, plump cakes called *petites madeleines* that look as though they have been molded in the grooved valve of a scallop shell. And soon, mechanically, oppressed by the gloomy day and the prospect of another sad day to follow, I carried to my lips a spoonful of the tea in which I had let soften a bit of madeleine. But at the very instant when the mouthful of tea mixed with cake crumbs touched my palate, I quivered, attentive to the extraordinary thing that was happening inside me, something isolated, detached, with no suggestion of its origin. And at once it rendered the vicissitudes of life unimportant to me, its disasters innocuous, its brevity illusory, acting in the same way love acts, by filling me with a precious essence; or rather this essence was not merely inside me, it was me. I had ceased now to feel mediocre, contingent, mortal. Where could it have come to me from, this all-powerful joy? I sense that it was connected to the taste of the tea and the cake, but it went infinitely far beyond it, could not be of the same nature. Where did it come from? What did it mean? How could I seize and apprehend it? I drink a second mouthful . . .

Contemporary fiction writers, enamored as we are with dialogue—how else to make it to the Academy Awards?—might have had the scene go something like this:

"You're cold," my mother said. "Would you like some tea?"

"No," I said. "You know I don't usually have tea, but okay. I guess I've changed my mind."

"Bring some tea for my son, please," she said. "I got some of those little cakes you used to like. You know, the ones shaped like scallop shells. Do you want one?"

"Okay," I said. "Might as well. It's such a gloomy day. Maybe I'll soak it in my tea."

"You used to do that when you were a kid."

"I remember. Sort of. But you know, it's a funny thing. The taste of it makes me feel weird."

"Really?"

"I can't figure it out."

"Well, you look weird. All of a sudden you look like you're in love or something."

"Yeah," I said. "The taste kind of makes me feel, I don't know, essential, not mediocre. I know it sounds crazy. It's just tea and soggy cake. Let me try another spoonful and see if I can figure it out."

"Good luck with that."

Certainly, the screenwriter can show the sense of touch—or at least show characters touching in all sorts of ways—but only the fiction writer can tell us how something feels, evoking through tactile associations not only pain or pleasure, but a distinct lifetime.

Consider Chekhov's "The Kiss":

His neck, round which soft, fragrant arms had so lately been clasped, seemed to him to be anointed with oil; on his left cheek near his moustache where the unknown had kissed him there was a faint chilly tingling sensation as from peppermint drops, and the more he rubbed the place the more distinct was the chilly sensation; all over, from head to foot, he was full of a strange new feeling which grew stronger and stronger.

I give credit to the director of 2013's *Gatsby* for his valiant attempt to preserve as much as possible Fitzgerald's language, his written words, through this premise of a therapeutic writing session. But of course, the bad news for Hollywood types who want all their rewards "up front" is that sometimes film just can't reproduce on the screen words that are meant for the page, for the silent communion of reader and writer.

In *Ulysses*, Leopold Bloom fills the kettle to make tea:

What in water did Bloom, waterlover, drawer of water, water-carrier, returning to the range, admire?

Its universality: its democratic equality and constancy to its nature in seeking its own level: its vastness in the ocean of Mercator's projection: its unplumbed profundity in the Sundam trench of the Pacific exceeding 8000 fathoms: the restlessness of its waves and surface particles visiting in turn all points of its seaboard: the independence of its units: the variability of states of sea: its hydrostatic quiescence in calm: its hydrokinetic turgidity in neap and spring tides: its subsidence after devastation: its sterility in the circumpolar ice caps, arctic and antarctic: its climatic and commercial significance: its preponderance of 3 to 1 over the dry land of the globe: its indisputable hegemony extending in square leagues over all the region below the subequatorial tropic of Capricorn: the multisecular stability of its primeval basin: its luteofulvous bed: its capacity to dissolve and hold in solution all soluble substances including millions of tons of the most precious metals: its slow erosions of peninsulas and islands, its persistent formation of homothetic islands, peninsulas and downwardtrending promontories: its alluvial deposits: its weight and volume and density: its imperturbability in lagoons and highland tarns: its gradations of colors in the torrid and temperate and frigid zones: its vehicular ramifications in continental lakecontained streams, and confluent oceanflowing rivers with their tributaries and transoceanic currents: gulfstream, north and south equatorial courses: its violence in seaquakes, waterspouts, artesian wells, eruptions, torrents, eddies, freshets, spates, groundswells, watersheds, waterpartings, geysers, cataracts, whirlpools, maelstroms, inundations, deluges, cloudbursts: its vast circumterrestrial ahorizontal curve: its secrecy in springs . . .

You know, you can't film that.

Not long after I returned from my glamorous dinner in New York, I got a phone call from the young producer. He had just had a great meeting with the Famous Director's agent, and everything was a go. Everyone was very excited. A few minor details to work out and the director and I could begin drafting the screenplay. Absolutely delighted, the young producer said as he hung up. Just delighted that this movie was going to happen.

And that was the last time we spoke.

Later I learned that the "few minor details" to be worked out included how many millions of dollars the Famous Director wanted to direct the film—all of it, of course, up front.

I was happily sunk into my own next novel by then, so I can't say I was disappointed. (In fact, a movie version of the novel—with voice-over—was eventually made by another young director/screenwriter who was gracious enough to keep me out of it. Except, I'm afraid, when he christened the novel's unnamed narrator "Alice.")

But I had also carried into the experience—the first-class trip from San Diego to New York, the limos, the lovely tea, and the expensive dinner in SoHo—some advice my agent had provided before these heady scenes unfurled.

What you need to know, and to keep in mind, she told me, is that every conversation in Hollywood begins like this: "'Hello,' he lied." Every word is a lie, even *hello*.

And that bit of exposition made all the difference.

THINGS

The intersection of Route 27 and Main Street in East Hampton, New York, has enchanted me since I was a child. There is the postcard loveliness of it: the town pond reflecting reeds and sky, the swans, the worn cemetery stones set in lush grass. Every summer of my childhood I felt that catch-your-breath thrill at the unchanging sight of it as my father drove us through the town for our two-week vacation in what we always called "the country," never "the Hamptons."

The sensation caught me again that day in late June when my husband and I returned to East Hampton after a ten-year hiatus. As we made the left turn into the village, I felt myself delighted once again by the placid beauty of the scene, the deep colors and the watery light. Passing the Home Sweet Home museum, a preserved cedar cottage from the 1700s, I recalled summer "educational" visits there and a fascination I'd had as a child with an antique checker set that was always on display—the checkers brown or yellow corn kernels, the board set up to suggest that a game was already underway, that the children who played it had only briefly, recently, stepped away.

My obsession with this display involved my certainty that someday, from the corner of my eye, I might actually catch a glimpse of the two children who had played there centuries ago—an obsession spiced deliciously by my absolute terror that I might, someday, actually catch, from the corner of my eye, a glimpse of the children who had played there, children now two hundred years dead.

As we drove through the village again that June, I recalled, as well, church fairs on the green and a delightful "needle in the haystack" game—delightful to me, who had no chance at games of skill—that involved simply searching through a pile of hay until you found a prize.

I remembered, too, an anniversary dinner my husband and I had shared, our fourth wedding anniversary thirty years earlier, at The Hedges Inn, just beyond the pond, where the bartender plied us with free drinks and ghost stories that involved innocent objects—an umbrella stand, a lady's shawl—moving eerily about the upstairs rooms.

That summer thirty years ago was also the summer of the year my father died, the first and last time my mother went out to the country alone.

Driving through the village once again, I was reminded that for me it had always been my father's place, East Hampton. He'd come out here from Manhattan as a child, brought by an Irish aunt who had married a local. He'd bought his first house on Dayton Lane. His older sister lived on Georgica Road. When we were children, it seemed to us that he knew everyone in town, from the policeman at Newtown Lane to the clerks at the A&P to the volunteers in the Ladies' Village Improvement Society shop—another, figurative, haystack for my brothers and me, where we were let loose every summer with a quarter or two to discover among the jumble all kinds of unexpected wonders, old picture books, ancient military medals, a cigar box filled with cat's-eye marbles, a brown paper bag brimming with odd buttons.

My husband and I were on our way to Amagansett, to a beach house we had rented years before. I was turning sixty and we were meeting old friends to celebrate, to commiserate. It struck me as we passed through the village that the years I'd had my father in my life—thirty—were now to be outnumbered by the years I was without him.

The single key was in its usual place at the Amagansett cottage, and once we let ourselves in, I found the two full sets of keys the owner had left for us. I placed one set on the mantel and was suddenly struck with the sixty-something premonition that we were going to lock ourselves out by week's end. I decided to put the other set in the car. I went out to the short driveway. The trunk was open. My husband was carrying our bags inside. I brushed aside a beach towel to place the keys in a secure corner of the trunk and suddenly saw my father's signature, as familiar as a much-loved face. I reached in. It was a Florida automobile-registration card, filled out with his last address, dated 1981, and signed with his own distinctive flourish. That car had been sold decades ago. This one was fairly new. For three years I'd opened and closed this trunk daily, filled it with grocery bags, suitcases, my mother's wheelchair. I'd never seen this card before. Nor had my husband. We had no idea why it was suddenly there.

Just before we left for that trip to Long Island, I was putting away the detritus of a completed novel—notebooks, drafts, galleys—when I found a poem I had copied out somewhere along the way, a poem written by the fictional Konstantin Perov in Nabokov's short story "A Forgotten Poet." I'd copied it down to remind myself of something—something about the way objects appear in fiction.

If metal is immortal, then somewhere
there lies the burnished button I lost
upon my seventh birthday in a garden.
Find me that button and my soul will know
that every soul is saved and stored and treasured

In *Swann's Way*, Proust tells the reader this:

I find the Celtic belief very reasonable, that the souls of those
we have lost are held captive in some inferior creature, in an
animal, in a plant, in some inanimate object, effectively lost to
us until the day, which for many never comes, when we happen
to pass close to the tree, come into possession of the object, that
is their prison. Then they quiver, they call out to us, and as soon
as we have recognized them, the spell is broken. Delivered by
us, they have overcome death and they return to live with us.

In *The Habit of Being*, her collected letters, Flannery O'Connor
says:

St. Augustine wrote that the things of the world pour forth
from God in a double way: intellectually into the minds of the
angels and physically into the world of things . . . The artist
penetrates the concrete world in order to find at its depths the
image of its source, the image of ultimate reality.

Whether they contain the souls of the dead or the image of
ultimate reality, no inanimate object (or animal or plant, for
that matter) in a story or a novel is arbitrary. How can it be?
It is not set there by nature or happenstance, by market forces
or human need. Objects in a novel or story are *created*, made

up, selected by a creative intelligence (the author), chosen and then hand-delivered via the prose, and as such they all, every one of them, quiver with meaning, or the potential for meaning. Every one of them contains the potential to stir a memory, evoke a metaphor, conjure a ghost, reflect an ultimate reality.

If Proust and O'Connor, and my own childish fear of haunted checkerboards, can't convince you of this, of the potential for meaning inherent in every object you include in your novel or story, think about it this way:

You receive a birthday gift from your partner, spouse, lover, oldest friend, whatever. It is, let's say, a ceramic chipmunk. Your first thought when you unwrap the gift is: Why? Was there some mad, perhaps drunken, moment from your past together that featured a chipmunk? Is there some classical or mythological or contemporary literary reference that you're missing? Doesn't the gift's very specificity—why not a ceramic rabbit or a Dutch boy or a pineapple—imply some message, some joke, some hidden meaning?

You look up from the gift to find that your friend is smiling warmly, knowingly. "Cute," you might say, "but what does it *mean*?"

If the explanation is good, as in, "If that chipmunk hadn't gotten into your tent at summer camp, we never would have met," if it evokes a forgotten past or connects cleverly to some aspect of your shared experience, your pleasure in the gift, and your admiration for your thoughtful friend, will increase dramatically.

If, however, your friend, partner, lover, spouse shrugs and says, "No meaning. I just bought it for you," you surely will be disappointed, nonplussed. You may even suspect that it has been regifted.

No object in a story or novel is arbitrary, because every object, every detail, in fact, is selected by the writer, who has chosen to notice it, to make note of it. Every detail *pours forth from the writer in a double way*: as something inevitable, because the world being described contains it, but also as something meaningful, because the writer has made note of it, selected it from all the physical objects existing in the world that he or she has chosen *not* to describe. And because it is chosen, selected, made note of, elevated by the author's attention above all objects that are not mentioned, purpose, meaning, an ultimate, creative intelligence, is implied.

And so all objects in fiction, even the most mundane, shimmer with mystery and meaning, with the souls of the dead as well as the image of some ultimate reality.

Burnished buttons or shell-shaped cookies, mummified remains in a museum's glass case or a mundane registration card from the Florida DMV, these objects are no longer simply the things themselves, but something transformed by the writer's attention, saved and stored and treasured by the writer's art.

REMEMBRANCE OF THINGS THAT NEVER HAPPENED: THE ART OF MEMOIR, THE ART OF FICTION

(First annual Frank McCourt Memorial Lecture, Sun Valley Writers' Conference, "Speak, Memory," 2019)

———

I t's a shopworn irony, as familiar to those of us who write fiction as it is to those who write memoir: somewhere in every crowd, there's a wary reader who will skeptically ask, Did this really happen?

When it is asked of novelists, the squinty-eyed implication seems to be: You didn't make this up, did you? It really happened, didn't it? It's not fiction at all, is it?

When the question is asked of the memoirist, the accusation gets turned on its head: You actually made this up, didn't you? It never really happened, did it? It's fiction, isn't it?

I have to confess that for many years I was that annoying reader when it came to my encounters with memoir. While reading any number of acclaimed titles, I found myself recalling a favorite expression of my Long Island youth: *Bullshit*. Or: Oh, come on. Really? You remember all this? You remember exactly where you were and what he said and what she said and what you ate and what you were wearing and how you were feeling—

I mean, really? Is your memory that good? Are your diaries that detailed? Aren't you sort of making this up?

No doubt a good deal of my own skepticism about the accuracy, the honesty of the memoir form arose out of my own experience as a young writer.

In 1972, I was a first-semester sophomore at Oswego State College—an outpost of the New York State university system on the edge of Lake Ontario—when I, tentatively, took my first creative-writing course, called The Nature of Nonfiction. Our initial assignment was to write a brief autobiographical essay—a memoir. I wrote about accompanying a frightened high school friend to a clinic in Queens where she had a very efficient, and legal, abortion. The essay was very sad. Very moving. And after our professor read it out loud to the class, he told me that I was indeed a real writer. Which was, of course, exactly what I longed to hear.

But what I didn't tell the professor was that nothing of what I'd described had actually happened. I had never accompanied a frightened high school friend to a clinic in Queens where she had an abortion. I had never reassured her as we went into the clinic together, struggling all the while with my own disapproval of what she was about to do, recalling as well what the nuns at school had told us about the killing of an unborn child (they break its limbs; they drown it in salt water). I didn't sit quietly in the crowded waiting room of that municipal health center, making note of the various women, of all ages and ethnicities, around me. (I had never, in fact, been inside a municipal health center.) I didn't see how the color had drained from my friend's face when the ordeal was finished. Nor did I cheer weakly when she showed me the pink packet of birth control pills the nurses had given her. I didn't comfort her gently when she broke down on the subway going home. I didn't, in fact, know who the "she" in the story was. I'd made her up.

I'd made it all up, including the "I" narrator, who, although she resembled me in age and ethnicity and geographic biography, wasn't me at all, since I never did a single thing she said she did, never felt what she felt, believed what she believed, saw what she saw.

And yet, as I listened to the professor read what I had written, I did see and hear and feel and believe. I saw how my lies, my fictional narrative, had become as vivid as any lived experience—as vivid for him, for me, for my fellow students there in a class called The Nature of Nonfiction, as if we had witnessed it all, lived it all, in real time, in real life. As if it was, indeed, nonfiction. As if I had told the truth.

"I got bad news for you, kid," the professor said when class had ended. I was certain he was going to tell me, You can't make stuff up. But what he said was, "You're a writer." And then he added, "And you'll never shake it."

At the time I thought what he meant by this addendum was that I would never shake the ambition, the sense of obligation, the urge—or whatever unshakable thing it is—that drives any person to pursue any art's uncertain path. But many, many years later, I've come to the conclusion that what he was trying to tell me was that I would never shake the addictive delight of seeing my words evoke a world, my words bringing the past—whether it's a real past or an imagined one—to vivid life. What's impossible to shake, he was trying to tell me, was the addictive delight of literary creation.

A delight that has brought me to realize, finally, that this whole question of actually lived or only imagined, of made-up or real, is completely irrelevant.

I can think of two writers, a fiction writer and a memoirist, who have helped lead me to this conclusion, and it's lovely that they are both evoked here today. One is Vladimir Nabokov, whose own memoir lends its title to the conference this year. The other is Frank McCourt, for whom this lecture is named.

Here's Frank McCourt in his second book, *'Tis*, describing a moment from his youth as an Irish émigré in a boardinghouse in New York City:

> If Mrs. Austin won't let me have a light I can still sit up in the bed or lie down or I can decide to stay in or go out. I won't go out tonight because of my bald head and I don't mind because I can stay here and turn my mind into a film about Limerick. This is the greatest discovery I've made from lying in the room, that if I can't read because of my eyes or Mrs. Austin complaining about the light I can start any kind of a film in my head. If it's midnight here it's five in the morning in Limerick and I can picture my mother and brothers asleep with the dog, Lucky, growling at the world and my uncle, Pat Sheehan, snorting away in his bed from all the pints he had the night before and farting from his great feed of fish and chips.
>
> I can float through Limerick and see people shuffling through the streets for the first Sunday Mass. I can go in and out of churches, shops, pubs, graveyards and see people asleep or groaning with pain in the hospital at the City Home. It's magic to go back to Limerick in my mind even when it brings the tears.

In the space of these two paragraphs, it seems to me, McCourt spans the divide between literary memoir and literary fiction. In the first paragraph, that film in his head is a home movie; it shows him what he knows, what he has experienced—his mother and brothers asleep, the dog growling, the uncle snorting after his great feed. It evokes moments conjured from recollection.

But in the second paragraph, as McCourt "floats through

Limerick"—something we can easily suppose he had never actually done or done only, perhaps, metaphorically—what he sees is born of recollection but not tied to it. He sees "people"—people in churches, shops, and pubs, people sleeping or groaning in pain. Not his mother or his brother or his uncle but the great wash of shuffling humanity going about their Sunday morning. In this second paragraph, recollection is given wings (he floats) by imagination, and had the young McCourt lying in his boarding-house bed chosen to float closer to any one of these shuffling people, to give any one of them a name, to follow any one of them through the streets of Limerick, seeking to determine just why they sleep or groan in pain, why they enter the church and not the pub, then this, his mind's journey back to Limerick, this film in his head, would pass seamlessly from memoir to fiction.

But the magic of it, of that ability to evoke the place, the people, the film, remains the same.

And here's Nabokov doing something similar in the pages of *Speak, Memory*, running that film in his mind—or, actually, with Nabokovian doubleness, running the film in his mind of himself as he runs a film in his mind about his mother:

> One day, after a long illness, as I lay in bed still very weak, I found myself basking in an unusual euphoria of lightness and repose. I knew my mother had gone to buy me the daily present that made those convalescences so delightful. What it would be this time I could not guess, but through the crystal of my strangely translucent state I vividly visualized her driving away down Morskaya Street toward Nevski Avenue. I distinguished the light sleigh drawn by a chestnut courser. I heard his snorting breath, the rhythmic clacking of his scrotum, the lumps of frozen earth and snow thudding against the front of the sleigh. Before my eyes and before those of my mother

loomed the hind part of the coachman, in his heavily padded blue robe, and the leather-encased watch (twenty minutes past two) strapped to the back of his belt, from under which curved the pumpkin-like folds of his huge stuffed rump. I saw my mother's seal furs and, as the icy speed increased, the muff she raised to her face—that graceful, winter-ride gesture of a St. Petersburg lady. Two corners of the voluminous spread of bearskin that covered her up to the waist were attached by loops to the two side knobs of the low back of her seat. And behind her, holding on to these knobs, a footman in cockaded hat stood on his narrow support above the rear extremities of the runners.

Still watching the sleigh, I saw it stop at Treumann's (writing instruments, bronze baubles, playing cards). Presently, my mother came out of this shop followed by the footman. He carried her purchase, which looked to me like a pencil. I was astonished that she did not carry so small an object herself, and this disagreeable question of dimensions caused a faint renewal, fortunately very brief, of the "mind dilation effect" which I hoped had gone with the fever.

As she was being tucked up again in the sleigh, I watched the vapor exhaled by all, horse included. I watched, too, the familiar pouting movement she made to distend the network of her close-fitting veil drawn too tight over her face, and as I write this, the touch of reticulated tenderness that my lips used to feel when I kissed her veiled cheek comes back to me— *flies* back to me with a shout of joy out of the snow-blue, blue-windowed (the curtains are not yet drawn) past.

The operative words here: *as I write this.*

It is the writing, the act of getting it down, that not only allows the "touch of reticulated tenderness" to fly back with "a shout of joy" out of the past; it is the writing that creates the touch, calls forth the joy.

That fake autobiographical essay I wrote all those decades ago at Oswego was not, of course, made up out of whole cloth. In 1970, three years before *Roe v. Wade*, New York was the first state to legalize abortion. Between 1971 and 1975, I was a student at an all-girl Catholic high school on Long Island, as were most of my friends, and of course the politics of abortion, so much in the news in those days, was also discussed in our classrooms. I had indeed heard our teachers describe for us the variety of procedures that could end a pregnancy: the cracked limbs and the salt water.

But we, my peers and I, were also coming of age in the era of sex, drugs, and rock and roll, in the aftermath of Woodstock, the waning of the Vietnam War, the first stirrings of feminism. The world that our teachers and our parents had thought they were preparing us for was not the world we found ourselves entering.

On the one hand, popular culture told us to rebel against the stifling strictures of the past; on the other, all of our personal resources—parental guidance, faith, prudence, and caution of all sorts—belonged to that past.

We were, in many ways, a generation caught in between, and many of the young women I knew back then suffered in that transition as 1970s-style sexual freedom left them with 1950s-style crises.

In my junior and senior years of high school, a kind of pregnancy epidemic swept through my extended social circles. Left to our own devices as we were, we girls shared, through whispered conversations, half-formed rumors, drunken confessions, what information we could glean about abortion laws and clinics in the city, about who had hastily left school to get married or whose peculiar weight gain had suddenly disappeared, about the various ways to trick your family doctor into giving you birth control (claim unpredictable periods, terrible menstrual cramps, bad skin or bad moods), about how to keep secret—from parents, from teachers, from boyfriends—what we were going through as we negotiated a future, a freedom, that no one had prepared us for.

There was something very plucky, very lonely, about these all-girl, underground networks of comfort, support, and information exchange, and no doubt it was some memory of that time, that lived experience, that inspired me to write, just a few years later, a faux memoir about accompanying a frightened friend into the faceless bureaucracy of a municipal health center for an efficient abortion.

A scene born of recollection but not tied to it. An experience I had felt, although I'd never lived it.

In his lovely short story "Spring in Fialta," Nabokov, in the guise of his fictional narrator, writes:

> I never could understand what was the good of thinking up books, of penning things that had not really happened in some way or other . . . were I a writer, I should allow only my heart to have imagination, and for the rest rely upon memory, that long-drawn sunset shadow of one's personal truth.

Of course we think of the imagination as the work of the intellect—Frank McCourt writes that it is magical to go back to Limerick in his mind—but how much more accurate it seems to credit the complex, imaginative magic of literary creation to the heart.

The poet Wallace Stevens writes in "A Postcard from the Volcano":

Children picking up our bones
Will never know that these were once
As quick as foxes on the hill;

And that in autumn, when the grapes
Made sharp air sharper by their smell
These had a being, breathing frost;

And least will guess that with our bones
We left much more, left what still is
The look of things, left what we felt

At what we saw . . .

In order to make a record of what we felt at what we saw, the literary artist—novelist and memoirist alike—must, of course, capture "the look of things." There must be detail, vivid detail—that great feed of fish and chips, that pink packet of birth control pills, the close-fitting veil drawn too tightly over the face.

There must be accuracy of place: the hospital at the City Home, the municipal health center, frozen St. Petersburg. The film that plays vividly in the mind's eye must be precisely focused, sharply described, real—whether *real* means actually existed or convincingly made-up.

But far more essential than this kind of accuracy is the emotional authenticity contained therein. Not simply the anthropologist's found object or the researcher's historical detail, not simply the thing itself, the thing observed—the setting, the object—but the thing transformed, utterly transformed, by the poet's eye, the heart's imagination, by what we felt at what we saw.

It is the obligation of "literary creation," Nabokov writes, "to portray ordinary objects as they will be reflected in the kindly mirrors of future times; to find in the objects around us the fragrant tenderness that only posterity will discern and appreciate in the far-off times when every trifle of our plain everyday life will become exquisite and festive in its own right . . ."

Consider this passage from Frank McCourt's *Angela's Ashes*:

We play games with Alphie and the pram. I stand at the top of Barrack Hill and Malachy is at the bottom. When I give the pram a push down the hill Malachy is supposed to stop it but he's looking at a pal on roller skates and it speeds by him across the street and through the doors of Leniston's pub where men are having a peaceful pint and not expecting a pram with a dirty-faced child saying Goo goo goo goo. The barman shouts this is a disgrace, there must be a law against this class of behavior, babies roaring through the door in bockety prams, he'll call the guards on us, and Alphie waves at him and smiles and he says, all right, all right, the child can have a sweet and a lemonade, the brothers can have lemonade too, that raggedy pair, and God above, 'tis a hard world, the minute you think you're getting ahead a pram comes crashing through the door and you're dishing out sweets and lemonade right and left, the two of ye take that child and go home to yeer mother.

Malachy has another powerful idea, that we could go around Limerick like tinkers pushing Alphie in his pram into pubs for the sweets and lemonade, but I don't want Mam finding out and hitting me with her right cross. Malachy says I'm not a sport and runs off. I push the pram over to Henry Street and up by the Redemptorist church. It's a gray day, the church is gray and the small crowd of people outside the door of the priests' house is gray. They're waiting to beg for any food left over from the priests' dinner.

There in the middle of the crowd in her dirty gray coat is my mother.

This is my own mother, begging. This is worse than the dole, the St. Vincent de Paul Society, the Dispensary. It's the worst kind of shame, almost as bad as begging on the streets where the tinkers hold up their scabby children, Give us a penny for the poor child, mister, the poor child is hungry, missus . . .

The door of the priests' house swings open and the people rush their hands out. I can hear them, Brother, brother, here, brother, ah, for the love o' God, brother. Five children at home, brother. I can see my own mother pushed along. I can see the tightness of her mouth when she snatches at a bag and turns from the door and I push the pram up the street before she can see me.

I don't want to go home anymore. I push the pram down to the Dock Road, out to Corkanree where all the dust and garbage of Limerick is dumped and burned. I stand a while and look at boys chase rats. I don't know why they have to torture rats that are not in their houses. I'd keep going on into the country forever if I didn't have Alphie bawling with the hunger, kicking his chubby legs, waving his empty bottle.

Mam has the fire going and something boiling in a pot. Malachy smiles and says she brought home corned beef and a few spuds from Kathleen O'Connell's shop. He wouldn't be so happy if he knew he was the son of a beggar. She calls us in from the lane and when we sit at the table it's hard for me to look at my mother the beggar. She lifts the pot to the table, spoons out the potatoes one each and uses a fork to lift out the corned beef.

It isn't corned beef at all. It's a great lump of quivering gray fat and the only sign of corned beef is a little nipple of red meat at the top. We stare at that bit of meat and wonder who will get it. Mam says, That's for Alphie. He's a baby, he's growing fast, he needs it. She puts it on a saucer in front of him. He pushes it away with his finger, then pulls it back. He lifts it to his mouth, looks around the kitchen, sees Lucky the dog and throws it to him.

There's no use saying anything. The meat is gone. We eat our potatoes with plenty of salt and I eat my fat and pretend it's that nipple of red meat.

The Dutch historian Johan Huizinga wrote about "our perpetual astonishment that the past was once a living reality," and I have come to believe that it is this astonishment that drives that skeptical reader, that would-be literary Inspector Clouseau, to ask, Did this really happen? Did Frank really remember that it was a friend on roller skates who distracted Malachy? Did the pram really crash through the doors of the pub? Did all this really occur on the same day? Does memory come to us in such a precise sequence? Who remembers so much, so clearly?

But it is this astonishment, as well, that makes the question irrelevant. In the writer's, the artist's, hands the past does indeed become a living reality, but a living reality infused—as it could not be, could never be, in the moment it is experienced, the moment in "real life"—with the fragrant tenderness that only posterity can discern. A living reality—a dirty pram, a snatched bag of food, a great lump of quivering gray fat—inseparable in its description, in its vivid depiction, from the emotion it evokes.

I would argue that there are no such moments in real life. The objects of our everyday existence, in real life, are just that. A bit of meat to a hungry child is just a bit of meat. It is only through the writing, the working at words, the storyteller's creation of context and character and sequence, the artist's selection of detail, that these moments are transformed within the films that play in our minds. Not merely emotion recollected in tranquility, but a created world infused with meaning—its very objects infused with meaning.

A meaning that the real world—where we are hungry or tired or distracted by the busyness of living—does not provide. That's the magic of it.

There's a story—apocryphal, perhaps—about the writer Bernard Malamud being confronted after a reading by an interrogating reader of the "Did this really happen?" sort. Malamud had just read from *The Natural*, and this reader took issue with the way the novel described a series of perfectly placed foul balls hit with full intention by Roy Hobbs, the novel's protagonist.

"Couldn't have happened," the reader said. "I'm a physicist, and the physics of it are all wrong." As the story goes, the audience, infected, no doubt, by the man's real-world credentials—a physicist, no less—looked warily to Malamud for his reply. There was a moment of skeptical silence. And then Malamud said, "Oh, but it really did happen!" A sigh of relief ran through the auditorium. Now the audience turned back to the man, once more taking the writer's side. "See?" they seemed to say. "It really did happen. Not made-up at all."

But then Malamud added, "It happened to the guy in my novel."

"We should always remember," Nabokov wrote, "that the work of art is invariably the creation of a new world . . . To call a story a true story is an insult to both art and truth."

A good twenty-plus years after I wrote that first, imagined tale of two young women—a cool narrator and her frightened friend—navigating those early days of reproductive freedom, I tried something like it again. I was in the midst of composing my sixth novel, *After This*. My intentions for this book had begun simply enough, inspired by some well-known lines from the poem "Nineteen Hundred and Nineteen" by W. B. Yeats:

> But is there any comfort to be found?
> Man is in love and loves what vanishes,
> What more is there to say?

In this book, I'd hoped to figure out, somehow or other, the silence at the end of those two rhetorical questions: Is there comfort to be found, Mr. Yeats? Is there more to say?

And so I set the novel in the time between post–World War II and post–Vietnam War, hoping the era would provide some sense not only of loss—of what vanishes—but of how we go on.

Writing this novel, then, writing about these postwar decades, brought me to consider once again the lives of the girls I'd known in the early seventies, friends and acquaintances who had been casualties of a swiftly changing culture. Considering those experiences once again—not as a tentative creative-writing student, but as a middle-aged woman, a mother, a novelist—I saw how the experiences of these girls had been paid scant attention.

Understandable, it seemed to me, given the fraught history of the times: the aftermath of the Vietnam War, the Watergate scandal, the continued struggle for civil rights, for human rights of all sorts. Given the "bigger" issues of those years, it is easy enough to argue that the lives, the dilemmas, the personal crises of some middle-class girls in a white-bread suburb who found themselves adrift, who found themselves "knocked up," were hardly worthy of the historian's, the dramatist's, the memoirist's, the novelist's attention, when so many larger, more terrible, more—let's face it—male-centered stories (War! Politics! Drug-running!) were taking place.

An unwanted pregnancy in the life of a teenage girl being—let's be honest—of limited interest to the larger population, since unwanted pregnancies of this sort happen only to teenage girls. Traumatic for her, sure, but in a girl way.

And even now we know how easily our culture, not to mention our courts, ignores the testimony, the trauma, of girls.

But memory, motherhood, and the latent contrariness that made me a novelist in the first place won out, as did the lives of my so-called ordinary characters as they sought whatever comfort is to be found amid life's inevitable losses.

And so, in *After This*, I tried again to give proper attention to the girls who had been caught up in those times, to the quiet, plucky, lonely, life-changing decisions they were forced to make.

This time, the two girls going to the abortion clinic in the city had names. And histories. And families. Historical context. Emotional context. This time, the frightened, pregnant friend was a smart, resilient young woman who'd had her first sexual encounter on a lark, for fun, and, perhaps, to find some relief from the sadness at home. Her beloved older brother has returned from Vietnam addicted, angry, emotionally wrecked. Her parents, who had raised their two children for a different world, are stunned by his transformation, confused and brokenhearted by the loss of him, and she—their good child, their loving daughter—will not burden them further with her small "girl" drama, her unwanted pregnancy. A young woman who has heard about all the ways an unborn child is murdered in the womb and yet chooses abortion out of love for her family, out of love for the living.

And then, because my own recollections told me that the times—those transitional, confusing, swiftly changing years— had produced a kind of epidemic of unwanted pregnancies among such middle-class girls, I imagined, as well, as the novel went on, another young woman with an unplanned pregnancy, yet another family devastated by the war, a young woman who makes, or is forced to make, a different choice.

Both characters are resilient, thoughtful, complex young women, caught between one world and another, neither one of them a "real" person out of my own, real-life experience, but each tied to memory nevertheless, formed by my heart's imagination and the long-drawn sunset shadow of personal truth.

And in recalling that novel, *After This*, I find myself recalling Frank McCourt.

I confess that I've been aware, since Frank's wife, Ellen, so generously invited me to deliver this lecture named for Frank, that "inside stories" about the man behind the memoirs might be expected. I think it's even hinted at in the description of this event, the promise that I would regale you with my memories of Frank McCourt. But honestly—if a fiction writer can ever claim to be honest—though Frank and I met a number of times, I didn't know him well. We never caroused together. I never sat in his classroom or drank with him at the Lion's Head. Not in "real life" anyway.

The first time I met Frank was at a literary conference in Galway, a conference that included a trip to the Aran Islands—to Inis Mór, the largest of the three islands—for an all-day, Woodstock-style series of open-air fiction and poetry readings inside the Druid fort that overlooks the ocean and the bay. And it is only in Nabokovian retrospect that the joy of that beautiful day returns to me—along with the astonishing fact that aboard that rocking ferry out to Inis Mór were Frank McCourt and William Kennedy, Michael Ondaatje, Dennis Smith, Edna O'Brien, and Joyce Carol Oates.

Only in retrospect can I consider that had that ferry gone down, perhaps fifty yet-to-be-written books—memoirs and novels—would have gone with it. Wait. Joyce Carol Oates. Perhaps a hundred yet-to-be-written books. A hundred stories. A hundred created worlds that would not have come into being, not because they hadn't happened in real life, but because they would not have been written into being. Sort of amazing.

Anyway, Frank and I met again, here and there. In 2006, he and I were backstage together at the Terrace Theater in the Kennedy Center. We were there for a fundraising event sponsored by a wonderful organization that was then known as Project Children.

At the time, Project Children sought to bring boys and girls, Protestant and Catholic, from Northern Ireland to the United States for a few weeks each summer so they might get to know one another, even become friends, away from the bitter divisions of their hometowns.

(In fact, an Irish friend recently suggested that the need now is for a similar program for the children of Democrats and Republicans, who could be brought from the United States to Belfast to learn how to get along with people they've been told to despise.)

The Kennedy Center fundraiser was an annual event for Project Children and usually featured a number of traditional Irish bands and dancers, as well as various inside-the-Beltway types—politicians and local celebs—reading Irish poetry or singing Irish songs.

But this year, the format had been changed a bit, made a bit more theatrical. A set had been built onstage—the replica of an Irish pub—and we "performers" were to come and go, singing or playing or reading from our work as if we were the denizens of some happy Irish village, just stopping by for a drink.

Backstage, there much subtle—and very Irish— winking and nodding about the absurdity of all this. For the "writerly" portion of the proceedings, Frank was to go out and charm the audience with his stories, as only Frank could do, and then he was to say something like, "Oh, now, here's Alice . . . ," and then I was to come onstage, pull up a barstool, and we two would chat for five minutes or so about all things Irish and Irish American. And then the next act would stop by.

But when we met backstage, Frank was carrying a copy of *After This*, which had been published just that year. He said he didn't want to talk about all things Irish or Irish American; he wanted to talk about my book, especially about the last pages, the ending. He pointed to the last line of the novel, grinning.

It was a line that led logically from the final scene, a scene that depicts the moments before a quiet, arranged wedding between that pregnant teen and her reluctant beau, as a young musician arrives to play the wedding march. But it was also a line that had invoked for me as I wrote it a motif I had only discovered while composing the novel, part of my own search for the answer to Yeats's question: Is there any comfort to be found?

Amid this vale of tears, the book posited, there is comfort in family, in the generosity of neighbors, in moments of unexpected grace delivered by strangers. There's also the comfort of art—the novel gives a nod to paintings and statues and buildings, to music and language. It acknowledges the comedic arts, as well: Laurel and Hardy, the Marx Brothers, Buster Keaton, and Harold Lloyd all get subtle, perhaps too subtle, nods in the pages of *After This*—as well as in that very last line, which contains one of those hidden double meanings that you write for your own amusement, quite certain no one else will ever get it.

But Frank got it. "W. C. Fields?" he asked me, pointing to the novel's last words.

In that final scene, a weary old priest listens as the young piano player, a stranger, a kid from Juilliard, gets a feel for the instrument in the empty church before the wedding:

> You would have to be a musician to explain the difference, but the priest knew it was there. There were the ordinary pianists who played, no doubt, as they had been taught to play, earnest, obedient, faithful to each note . . . , and then there was a kid like this, who played in a trance, eyes closed, transformed, transported, inspired (that was the word), not the engine for the instrument but a conduit for some music that was already there, that had always been there, in the air, some music, some pattern, sacred, profound, barely apprehensible, inscrutable, really, something just beyond the shell of earth and sky that had always been there and that needed only this boy, a boy like this, to bring it briefly, briefly, to his untrained ear.
>
> Something he hadn't even known he'd been straining to hear.

The priest then asks the pianist if he's taken a lot of lessons. The boy responds that he's taken a lot of lessons, but it seems he's always known how to play.

The novel concludes with the old priest's words, "It's a gift, then."

"*It's a Gift*," I told Frank, "W. C. Fields's best movie."

Frank grinned. "I knew it!" he said, as pleased by this bit of writerly subterfuge as if he and I had conspired to include it.

"To hell with the producers," he said. "Let's go out there and have a real conversation."

This was not at all what I had anticipated or prepared for, but I knew by then that you couldn't be in Frank McCourt's presence for more than a minute before you came to believe that whatever he proposed, whatever he was about to say or do, would not only be spontaneous and surprising and utterly marvelous, but great fun.

I recall that Joanie Madden, the premier Irish flute player and founder of the band Cherish the Ladies, who was backstage with us, turned to me when she heard Frank's rebellious plan. "God help you," she said.

When my cue came, I strolled out onto the stage, into the "pub," and perched myself on the barstool beside Frank's. As promised, he asked me to read the last few pages of *After This*.

And when I finished, Frank was off, talking about language, detail, the arc of a story, the art of an ending. He's an angel, isn't he? Frank said of the young musician who appears in the last scene, an angel bringing the gift of music to this broken family? Yes, I said. And when did you know that's what he was? he asked.

He leaned forward on the barstool, like a man leaning into the wind on the back of a horse that was gathering speed, and I glimpsed then the wonderful "teacher man" that he had been: inquiring, encouraging, delighted by the charms he saw in everyone, delighted by story, delighted by words.

It's about all the things we take comfort from in the mad and hurtful world, Frank said. Family, faith, music, art. Laughter especially.

We went on, about inspiration and surprise and the thrill of discovering what you didn't know you knew but always somehow knew you knew—as the priest does—through the careful and dogged, wonderful and terrible, working at words. Words. Stories. Memories. Imagination.

Five minutes of this and the poor producer at the foot of the stage was making the "wrap it up" sign. Frank flashed the audience that grin of his and then told them, He wants us to stop, but we're not stopping. I'm enjoying this. There's so much to say.

We were on a stage at the Kennedy Center, perched on barstools that had never been in a bar, in a plywood pub with not a bit of Guinness on tap, no drink at all, pretending to be two old friends chatting casually, when actually, in reality, our sole purpose here was to raise some money for a very good cause. And yet, in those ten minutes we spent talking, all that artifice, all those good intentions, not to mention the producer, the audience, the "real" time and the "real" place, as well as the artificial one, fell away, and we became, authentically, honestly, just two writers, two readers, talking about what matters most: memory, heart, words, the film in the mind, the magic of literary creation.

What I'm trying to tell you, dear readers, is this: Why ask, "Did this really happen?" Why insult both art and truth? Sit down. Sit back. Forget everything that twirls its hands and tells you, "Move on. Wrap it up." Take a deep breath. There's so much to say. Let the film run in your mind; cherish it. It will bring comfort even if it brings the tears.

What I'm trying to say in Frank's memory is: Embrace the astonishing reality of a vivid world, a created world, formed only of words on a page. It's a gift.

FINALLY

The novelist Thomas Williams was my first teacher in the graduate writing program at the University of New Hampshire. Tom was a gentle soul—thoughtful, kind, generous—a marvelous line-by-line editor with, at middle age, a solid body of critically acclaimed work to his credit, including a National Book Award for his novel about the writing life, *The Hair of Harold Roux.*

Tom appeared one evening at a graduate-student party looking like a man washed up onshore. He had just received an early copy of a major review of his latest novel, which was based on stories he'd once told his children. He'd been "eviscerated," he said, by another, more famous, fiction writer—a writer he'd considered, until this moment, a friend. We, his students, carried him cups of beer. We gathered around him. He was stunned, angry, mournful, brokenhearted. He told us that at this stage of his career, there was no recovering from such a review.

We, knowing nothing, tried to reassure him. He had an illustrious publishing record. He had a National Book Award. He had pursued his art with dedication and seriousness. Given his life to it. Surely, one complaining review . . .

He looked at us—I think of how young and earnest we must have seemed—and everything in his face and his manner and his pained smile said, "If you can do anything else, kids, do it."

For many years, my literary agent was also Saul Bellow's literary agent. Harriet regularly collected from the public sphere any slights or jibes or whiny critical assessments directed at her most famous client, in part to shield him from them, in part to be offended on his behalf. She would always share these with me. I remember asking her, only half facetiously, "Shouldn't there be a statute of limitations on snide comments about wonderful writers, some rule that says that after so many great novels, or after a Nobel Prize, no dissenting views are allowed?"

"The idiots," Harriet said, "will always want the last word."

Once, she had me sit with her in her office while we listened on speakerphone to his publisher's lawyer, who was grilling Bellow about a short story he had written, sniffing for any possible case for libel. The lawyer went through every line of the story, every character, every incident, asking over and over again: "Is this true? Is this a real person? Did this really happen?" Bellow answered patiently, politely, even graciously—"No, that didn't happen. Yes, I had a cousin once . . ."—while I grew angrier and angrier. This great man, this great writer, this artist and his art being subjected to the indignity of such banal nitpicking? I looked across the desk to Harriet. She shrugged, and her shrug said, "This is what it's like. This is the writing life." She pointed to the phone: Bellow, his voice weary now, betraying his age, was thanking the man for his time—thanking him, when surely it should have been the other way around. *If you can do anything else*, I heard, *do it*.

As an adjunct lecturer at the University of California, San Diego, I was delighted with the prospect of encountering Robert Stone, who was a visiting writer that year. He proved elusive until one afternoon toward the end of the semester when I stepped out of my office at the same moment that Robert Stone stepped out of his. The corridors of the building that housed us were long and bleak and starkly white. It was late in the day, and there wasn't another soul around. He saw me. I saw him. There was nothing to be done. Nervously, I approached him down the length of that long, empty corridor—I was pretty sure that if he'd had the chance to run, or evaporate, he would have—and introduced myself, stammering about how much I admired his novels, hoping to add that I'd been a student of Thomas Williams, whose *Hair of Harold Roux* had shared that National Book Award with Stone's *Dog Soldiers*.

But he cut into my blather. "What are you working on?" he demanded.

I said I was just about to publish my second novel.

He shuddered—physically shuddered—and threw up his hands. "Second novel!" he shouted without meeting my eye. "The second novel's a killer."

And then he swiftly turned, went back into his office, and shut the door. I stood alone for a moment in that bleak corridor, utterly bereft, terrified.

If you can do anything else, I tell aspiring writers now, if you can do anything other than pursue this literary fiction thing and still sleep at night and wake joyful in the morning and know that the hours of your days have been well spent, then you should do that—that other thing.

The beauty of the advice is how quickly it clarifies, for some of us, what we've always known: Of course we can't. We can't.

number to its director, Wyatt Prunty, so I might receive an invitation to teach there next summer. "I think you'll enjoy it."

"Of course," I said—as you do, when God calls. Although, looking at my temporarily silenced brood (was the baby about to wail? was the oldest only pretending to strangle himself? where was my daughter heading with that uncapped magic marker?), I thought: Impossible.

Which is what I told Wyatt when the call came. "No problem at all," Wyatt said. "Your family is most welcome."

I'm forever grateful to Wyatt Prunty and to the Sewanee Writers' Conference for that warm welcome, extended to me, and to my family, summer after summer for more than twenty years. Many of these thoughts about the art of fiction would have remained just that—silent theories expounded while brushing my teeth, or improvised riffs offered in the casual give-and-take of writing workshops—were it not for the formal craft lectures I was asked to deliver at Sewanee.

I am grateful, too, to the many brilliant students and generous colleagues, especially those in the Writing Seminars at Johns Hopkins University, who have tolerated my improvised riffs, and who have, in turn, inspired, informed, amended, and expanded these various notions regarding our craft and sullen art. It's been my privilege to be in your company.

And, as always, my thanks to Sarah Burnes and Jonathan Galassi.

ACKNOWLEDGMENTS

It wasn't God on the phone, but close enough. Although surely even God could not have conveyed so much affection and warmth in such a simple greeting:

"Hello, Alice. This is Bob Giroux. I hope I'm not interrupting your writing."

It was early August in the swampy environs of suburban Washington, D.C. That terrible season of mind-numbing stasis. Summer camps had ended, and our family's annual vacation trip to Maine had not yet begun. My three children, ages nine, six, and one and a half, were at the kitchen table. They were finishing a late breakfast, watching cartoons, talking, fighting, complaining, cranky with too much summer.

Tethered to the wall phone, I swiped violently at the air to silence them. Fingers to lips. Finger across the throat. Unholy motherly grimace.

"Hello, Mr. Giroux," I said calmly. "How nice to hear from you." Robert Giroux of Farrar, Straus and Giroux, the storied publishing house that had become, by some fateful sleight of hand on the part of my editor, Jonathan Galassi, *my* publishing house. Robert Giroux, editor of T. S. Eliot, George Orwell, Virginia Woolf, Flannery O'Connor, Jack Kerouac, Susan Sontag, Bernard Malamud, Isaac Bashevis Singer, Nadine Gordimer, Derek Walcott, Seamus Heaney. Bob Giroux just calling casually on an August morning, hoping not to interrupt my writing, calling to say he'd just returned from a delightful visit to the Sewanee Writers' Conference at the University of the South, in Tennessee, and would I mind terribly if he gave my phone

PERMISSIONS ACKNOWLEDGMENTS